...AND IT JUST GETS SILLIER!

heat The Annual 2007 Contents

Welcome!

12 beauty things
you can't live without

GORGEOUSNESS GUARANTEED. NO MATTER WHAT YOU WERE UP TO LAST NIGHT

Frozen hearts by Jade Goody

The best-selling author gives us a touching tale of haddock and heartache. Yes, really!

"He said he was from East Angular"

"He told her that he liked the smell of fish"

TOP TORSOS 2007

PETE BURNS

WE SAID: "Using genitalia as the focal point of your look is brave, even when your waxer is this good. But a surgical-stocking encased scrotum can't distract from a condom-encased limb. And what's with the wires? A nicotine drip? Catheter?"

He says:

"Fuck off you bastards, you know nothing about fashion."

SU POLLARD

WE SAID: "Colour-blind, car-crash combos are Su's thing, but looking like you've been attacked by a bunch of five-year-olds with Magic Markers is taking it too far. Rather fetching amphibian accessory, though."

She says:

"I adore this outfit: it says, 'I'M ALIVE.' I'm the original accessory queen, hence the hairclips, belts and necklace. I think you'll find that almost all the colours in my 'car-crash' combo match, and as for the 'Magic Marker' comment, I'd be thrilled if a five-year-old had the talent to produce an artwork of such glorious magnitude."

TH
Stars

WHAT WERE YOU INKING?

fight back!

The *WWYT* pages strike fear into the hearts of any badly dressed celeb. 2006's worst offenders now explain their hideous outfits

KATE GARRAWAY (AT EIGHT-MONTHS PREGNANT)

WE SAID: "Best tread carefully when commenting on a mum-to-be's maternity wear, but there's no need to don vomit-splattered gear before the nine months are up."

She says:

"OK, it's a fair cop. But by that stage in my pregnancy, I was just glad to find anything that buttoned up! Blame it on my hormones. The coat was a present and I have worn it since, but looking at that picture again I may have to think twice next time!"

KINGA

WE SAID: "Stripes are tricky unless you're eight or in an 80s horror film. Kinga's got the horror bit, but even the wide-eyed look can't distract from her inside-out top and sock/tights combo."

She says:

"I love this outfit! Mum bought me the socks from Borehamwood market because they reminded her of Alicia Silverstone in *Clueless*. I saw Jordan wearing an inside-out stripy top like this one and couldn't believe it when I found mine on eBay for £7, including P&P. I think I looked beautiful. I haven't worn it since, though."

CARLEY STENSON

WE SAID: "The whiff of a red-carpet bash turns the *Hollyoaks* female cast into dogs' dinners. This pastel perversion might look sweet on a five-year-old, but a grown woman?"

She says:

"I take offence at the five-year-old child comment. That night I wanted to wear something different because I always play safe. I picked this dress from Strawberry Tarts in Liverpool. I liked it because it was sweet, and not too revealing, so there was a method behind my madness!"

TAMARA BECKWITH

WE SAID: "Tamara was on *Dancing On Ice*, now her legs look covered in it. Tamara, you may want to milk your dance fame, but by stealing other contestants' costumes? Hmm."

She says:

"I was mighty unsure of the ensemble myself. I was actually off to a 'metallic' theme fancy-dress party. I love the Dolce & Gabbana dress and I already had these tights at home. I popped the white faux-fur jacket on and possibly went overboard, but it was definitely a talking point!"

GEMMA ATKINSON

WE SAID: "Maybe Gemma is trying to distract us from her awful haircut. After all, who will look at your head if you wear a gynaecologically revealing skirt and bosom-strangling corset?"

She says:

"I thought I looked good, but I did get dressed with two friends while downing vodka shots! I had to wear a corset as I'd just had a boob job and the doctor had advised me to wear support. No excuse for the skirt. I think my hair looked fab, but no, I'll never wear that look again!"

KIMBERLEY WALSH

WE SAID: "Why is Kimberley the colour of tan leather from top-to-toe? Take a tip from us, Kim: skin and outfit should never match, especially not when your shade of choice is so, well, faecal."

She says:

"OK, I hold my hands up: the look as a whole is not good. But without the jacket, it does look good. I was leaving the club and it was cold, so I put on the jacket, which was a mistake. Sadly, once you've had one too many mojitos, you do lose your fashion sense…"

KATE LAWLER

WE SAID: "Nothing says cheap quite like the colours red and black together. Kate has, however, diverted attention with her trainee-stylist fringe and kangaroo-testicle scarf."

She says:

"I liked my outfit – but when I saw that picture, the scarf didn't look all that. Kangaroos' nuts are a big no-no. I got my black skinny jeans from Topshop, black shirt from Karen Millen and the boots from Office. The belt is my mum's. And I think black and red *do* go together."

The Nosey Parker Interview

Kerry Katona

Where are you now and what are you doing?
I'm sat eating a bagel on-set, making a new Iceland advert. I'm with my staff, make-up artist and hairdresser, on a break during filming. Now I've got this baby bump, it looks even better in the adverts – I come across as a right mumsy mum… or like I've eaten a trolley load of food!

What are you like in a strop?
I don't really get in strops. I'm not one to throw chairs or pull hair or anything. I'm not that bad. Contrary to what people think, I just go quiet and get a bit agitated.

How much do you weigh?
Ten stone – but I am pregnant! I love being pregnant. I can eat whatever I want and not worry about whether I'll see dodgy pictures of me in the papers stuffing my face with a hamburger. I'm eating for two now and it's great. Mark [Kerry's fiancé] loves a bit of extra "me" to cuddle, so I won't be stressing about losing weight quickly after I have the baby. I'm not like all those other celeb mums – I'm going to embrace my baby fat!

Where's the weirdest place you've ever had sex?
In a caravan, recently. No one saw the caravan a rockin'… Well, I think no one did! And it *was* with Mark, by the way. He's just so wonderful – in all areas!

What was the last call you avoided?
To tell the truth, I avoid most of my phone calls. I don't like answering my mobile cos I always worry it'll be bad news. I only really answer the phone to the kids and Mark. And to Max [Clifford, Kerry's publicist]… most of the time!

What body hair do you remove?
All of it except on my head! I wouldn't be seen dead with a hairy armpit or a few strays poking out of my bikini, but I do worry, what with being pregnant and all, that I won't be able to sort it out down there for when the baby comes.

What's your middle name?
Jane Elizabeth. Jane after my stepsister and Elizabeth after my nan.

Who was the last person to tell you off?
Probably Max. He's always telling me off for something. But I'm used to it and know he has my best interests at heart.

How often do you change your bed sheets?
I don't change my bed sheets; my nice cleaner does it.

What pants are you wearing?
I'm wearing a white thong at the moment, but my favourite style is French knickers. I probably change my undies roughly twice a day. Oh, but I don't mean roughly as in rough!

What does your best mate do for a job?
Mark is my driver and he's my best friend. He's dead happy about the new baby. We're hoping for twins cos they run in his family. I'd be over the moon if that happened, but we'll just wait and see!

Tongues in public. Discuss.
I don't mind a bit of tongue action in public, whether it's me or anyone else! Although, now I think about it, I'm not sure why I do it; it just happens. It just falls out of my mouth. I don't like seeing school kids going for it down the bus stop, though. It makes me think of my own two little girls snogging for England one day and that does my head in.

"I wouldn't be seen dead with a hairy armpit"

PROFESSIONAL CHICKEN
We're sure he still looked very handsome while doing it, but one of Brad's first jobs was standing outside the eaterie El Pollo Loco in LA, dressed in a chicken outfit. "I wound up in a giant chicken costume, clucking, trying to lure customers into a fast food restaurant," he recalls. Things could have been so different...

Geri Halliwell
GAME-SHOW HOSTESS
Before Geri spotted *that* ad for a five-piece girl band in *The Stage*, she earned a crust as a game-show hostess on Turkish TV (like you do). "They wanted a girl who looked half decent, but with some personality, and it was great," she says. "They flew me out there every weekend."

Jobs befo
wer

They have megabucks careers now, but back in the day these stars had *very* different professions

Rod Stewart GRAVEDIGGER

Before highlighting his hair and becoming a sex god for mums everywhere, young Rod worked for six years as a gravedigger in Highgate Cemetery in north London. That really is a dead-end job for you....

Johnny Depp PEN SALESMAN

After a stint trying to make it big as a rock star, Johnny left Florida for LA, lived in his car and supported himself by selling pens over the telephone. In 1983 he bagged his first film role in *Nightmare On Elm Street*, saying, "I would have done anything because I was a phone solicitor, selling pens and making about $25 a week."

Madonna DOUGHNUT SELLER

While making a bid for stardom, Madge paid the rent with a job in the Times Square branch of Dunkin' Donuts in New York. "Just one squeeze per doughnut," her supervisor used to tell her. Seems she was a little heavy handed, though – she was eventually sacked for squirting jam over a customer.

re they
e famou$

Robbie Williams
DOUBLE-GLAZING SALESMAN

Before Robbie became the most famous man on the planet, his days were spent in his hometown of Stoke, selling double glazing door-to-door. Thing is, he wasn't too hot at it. Part of Rob's technique was to tell potential punters how bad the company was!

Mariah Carey
SWEEPER IN A BEAUTY SALON

"The manager wanted every female working there to have a cute, phony name, like Foxy or Stormy," Mariah remembers. "He decided I would be 'Echo' and kept asking, 'What's your name again?' I told him, 'It's Mariah.' And he said, 'No – now it's Echo.' So I said, 'Excuse me, I have to make a phone call', and I never went back.'

Kerry Katona
WORKED IN A CHIPPIE

At 16, Kerry had flogging fish down to a fine art at her local chippie in Warrington. "I could wrap a bag of chips with my eyes closed," Kerry proudly reveals. "I was very generous – I think that's why I was so popular."

Vic Reeves
PIG FARMER
Before comedy came calling, Vic was a pig farmer. The lucky lad says he "swilled out 100 grunters at a time" and also, erm, castrated the pigs "to stop them going mad. We'd ride on the pigs' backs until we fell off and then climb on the silage," he confesses.

Orlando Bloom
CLAY-PIGEON TRAPPER
Age 13, the Hollywood star once spent a summer slogging his guts out on a pigeon-shooting range. "I was a clay trapper," he says. "People would go clay-pigeon shooting on the weekends, and when they said 'pull', I was the one who released the pigeon. It was wild." Orlando obviously didn't get out much back then.

Dermot's surviving

Hate mince pies? R...
much. Luckily, Mr O'...

DON'T do your Christmas shopping too early. Wait until the final few days before buying your presents, that way you get into the spirit of things. Go late-night shopping, get all excited and eat those horrible burnt chestnuts from the man on the street corner. Whatever you do, make a night of it. If I had my way, they wouldn't be able to put any Christmas gifts or adverts out until the first Sunday of Advent – I'm not interested in Christmas in October. Bah, humbug!

DO put a stocking at the end of your bed because you'll get more gifts. I don't care if I'm in my 30s. Sadly, my mum is still under the assumption that tangerines or clementines make good Christmas presents. How the heck do you feign excitement when you pull out one of those? Soft fruit does not have the same impact as a Scalextric. Fact.

DON'T get sucked into girly shops and tricked into buying weird presents. Steer clear of make-up nonsense and cucumber hangover things for eyes that make you think, "Ooh, they'll like that." You'll only open the bathroom cabinet a year down the line and see they haven't been touched. I never learn, though – this year I've bought some funny towel hair turbans for my sister and girlfriend Dee. I keep looking at them and questioning my masculinity.

guide to
g Christmas

with the parents already? Sometimes the festive season can be too
is on hand with his top tips for a perfect Yuletide

DON'T go to the pub you always went to in your younger days on Christmas Eve, because you'll probably find it isn't full of your friends any more. Most of them have moved away from home and the pub's now rammed with 15-year-olds from the school you used to go to.

DO get a little bit merry at home that night nstead (my fave winter ipples are bitter or a nice dark pirit like rum), but not so merry you get chucked out of midnight Mass, which is what happened to a couple of my riends once. Being drunk in hurch probably isn't the right hing to do. I usually stand at e back and sway around a lot. hen I feel guilty because I can't emember much afterwards.

DON'T go for a repeat prescription n Christmas Eve: ie, pulling an x-girlfriend. You're always going regret it. Really.

DO get up early on Christmas morning so you can enjoy e whole day. I used to jog with my ates at 8am every Christmas Day e to a bet we made. That kept ing for about five years until one them had kids and realised they ould possibly be at home for their ild's first Christmas. w I have no one run with... Sob.

DO offer to help your parents in the kitchen on Christmas Day, but make sure you time your offer correctly. The best time to pipe up is when your mum's already in the middle of doing things and won't want to delegate. Avoid speaking up when lunch is almost ready, though, or you may hear the dreaded words, "Yes, love, you can set the table."

DO pour your dad a Buck's Fizz on Christmas morning, top up his glass all day and tell him it's just orange juice. It's nice to see your parents get a bit tiddly and hear them repeat the same stories all day. Plus, you get more hugs.

DON'T rely on the telly to entertain you during the Christmas holiday. It's far too risky, so make sure you always have a back-up plan in the form of a few of your favourite festive DVDs. For me, you can't go wrong with a black-and-white war classic – *Where Eagles Dare* is my personal recommendation. And Christmas just wouldn't be the same without a good musical. I love *Oliver!* although it seems to go from winter to summer in five minutes, which slightly freaks me out.

DO buy an alternative Christmas album. Forget all these new Top Xmas Ringtones gubbins. My all-time three favourite Yuletide tracks are as follows: *Pipes Of Peace* by Paul McCartney – I loved the World War One-style video (and often imagine it in my head). Next, *A Winter's Tale* by David Essex. I loooove that song. I'm actually welling up thinking about it now. My favourite line is: "The snow has covered all your footsteps and I can follow you no more..." It's very sad. But that's the whole point. And lastly, *O Little Town Of Bethlehem* sung by the underrated Cliff Richard. I do a very good impression, by the way, but sadly you can't hear it because you're reading this.

DO go for a brisk afternoon walk on Christmas Day. It's the one day of the year people are allowed to say hello to each other without it being weird. And you don't have to ask to pet someone's dog, which is nice.

DO play games. We're Trivial Pursuiters in our family. Problem is we only have the 1970 edition, which doesn't make for many right answers in our household. "Which swimmer won the 1954 Olympics?" Eh? My dad's the worst cheat in the world, too. He thinks it's funny.

These pics of Mariah aren't as identical as they seem – can you find the ten differences?

A

B

How did you do?
Find the answers on **page 125**

The Nosey Parker Interview

Russell Brand

PAUL RIDER

Where are you now and what are you doing?
I'm here in north London, talking to you, waiting to have my photos done for the *heat* interview. I'm enjoying it, it's nice, except your constant grilling about my private life.

What are you like in a strop?
Shouty and petulant. I'm not one for being insular and sulking. I was like it this morning when the cab driver sat outside my house for half an hour without telling me he'd arrived.

How much do you weigh?
Twelve, 12½st. I was bulimic when I was a teenager. I was fat, I was bullied for being fat, I was told, "You're fat!", and I played Fat Sam in *Bugsy Malone*. The word "fat" kept coming up. So I try not to eat too much, but last night I had a cheese and mushroom omelette, chips, onion rings, vanilla milkshake and sticky toffee pudding delivered. At midnight.

What's the weirdest place you've ever had sex?
Umm… Up a hill, in a tree, in a lift, on a train… The hill was a place called Arthur's Seat in Edinburgh. I didn't go up there in order to have sex – I wouldn't want to cheapen the walk, which was bloody good, too.

What was the last call you avoided?
Lots! I used to give my number to anyone, then get strange calls from odd people at 4am. I'm not giving out my number so willy-nilly now, so I avoid lots of calls. In fact, there's only about five people I answer to.

What body hair do you remove?
None! But it's good manners to trim your pubic hair. I don't remove it, though, I cultivate it. Prune it, nurture it. One of the papers said I shave my ballbag, which was strange. Someone did it to me once, but it's dangerous – you have to pull it taut and rake a razor up it. But women are more inclined to pop it in their gobs, so there is an upside.

What's your middle name and where is it from?
Edward. There's no reason for it. I like it, though, because my initials are REB, rebel.

Who was the last person to tell you off?
Probably Chip, who runs Focus, the rehabilitation centre I went to. He's always telling me to concentrate on what I'm doing and stop being an idiot. Stop larking around with girls.

How often do you change your bed sheets?
Once a week. Is that normal? I have two sets of bed linen on rotation, but I might get more.

What pants are you wearing?
Y-fronts. People laugh at them, but they're brilliant. Plain, neat, white Y-fronts. I kept getting ridiculed, so I thought I'd go down to Soho to buy some sexy ones. They were black and tight, with another layer to put your ballbag through to make your pouch more prominent. But they just hurt. They scoop up your nuts.

What does your best mate do for a job?
My best mates are Karl Theobald the comedian, who's Martin Dear in *Green Wing*, and Matt Morgan who writes with me at MTV and does the 6Music radio show.

Tongues in public. Discuss.
Without them, language would suffer terribly. We would have to communicate through tears and semaphore. So I think tongues are vital in public. If, as I suspect, the question means kissing in public, well, sometimes you're in love and you can't help it.

"One of the papers said I shave my ballbag"

Guess W

BRIT SINGER
1. He's the proud dad of a daughter called Tianie-Finn
2. One of his best mates is Tara Palmer-Tomkinson
3. He first found fame in a colourful boyband

The dodgy haircuts, the unfortunate outfits, the goofy grins... Who'd have guessed this lot would grow up into some of the most groomed and glam stars in Celebville. But can you tell who these little poppets are?

ho?

POSH BRIT ACTRESS
1. Her breakthrough film role was in Kenneth Branagh's *Much Ado About Nothing*
2. She spent nine hours getting her hair done for this year's MTV Movie Awards
3. Her actor dad died when she was just six

FAMOUS DAUGHTER
1. Her middle name is Garry
2. She has a son called Ryder
3. Her mum is a super-famous Hollywood actress

TV PRESENTER
1. He's a massive Arsenal fan
2. He's Irish through and through
3. He started out on *T4*

SEXY ACTOR
1. He started out in ill-fated soap *Families*
2. He famously had a bit of bother with his children's nanny
3. He's named after a Beatles song

POP RUDE GIRL
1. This feisty lady's real name is Alecia Beth Moore
2. She joined Lil' Kim, Maya and Christina Aguilera for one of her hits
3. Her pop name comes from a character in *Reservoir Dogs*

SKINNY ACTRESS
1. Her marriage lasted four months
2. She made big pants cool again
3. She used to date Jack White from The White Stripes

HOLLYWOOD HEART-THROB
1. He was born on 11 November 1974
2. He loves a Brazilian
3. He became a major movie star after his 1996 role in *Romeo + Juliet*

BAD-BOY RAPPER
1. He has a tattoo of his daughter on his right shoulder
2. His middle name is the very unglamorous Bruce
3. He married and divorced his wife twice

TV FUNNYMAN
1. His wife is famous for her pink hair
2. One of his best mates is Ricky Gervais
3. He has a daughter is called Betty Kitten

COCKNEY ACTRESS
1. This bubbly blonde knows how to pull a good pint
2. She starred in several cheeky British films in the 60s and 70s
3. You can't mistake her naughty laugh

GEEKY ACTOR
1. He's got lots of Friends in the TV world...
2. ...One is a monkey called Marcel
3. He used to go out with Natalie Imbruglia

How did you do?
Find the answers on **page 125**

PHOTOLIBRARY.COM; REX FEATURES; SCOPE; SPLASHNEWS.COM; WENN.COM

The Nosey Parker Interview

Richard & Judy

Where are you now and what are you doing?

Judy: We're in my dressing room. We've just finished filming the show with McFly and Nikki from *Big Brother*.

Richard: We'll head home after this, might stop off on the way for a drink.

What are you like in a strop?

R: If it's a little strop, I shout; if it's big I go quiet.

J: He does get very stroppy. He stamps around.

R: But we don't get stroppy with each other. Our rows are usually stupid. I'll say something to Judy like, "You shouldn't have said that to so-and-so!" and she'll say, "I didn't!" and I'll say, "You did!"

How much do you weigh?

R: About 12st.

J: I'm about three-and-a-half ounces! We don't obsess about our weight.

Where's the weirdest place you've ever had sex?

R: On an old passenger ship in Preston docks, called The Flying Star (as opposed to "The Flying Fuck"). During a break we went for food, and then to our cabin… for a flying fuck!

J: It was in the 80s!

What was the last call you avoided?

J: I never take calls because I've got a phobia about answering the phone. I get all nervous…

R: I'm always ignoring calls to the house because they're always for the kids. There's no point answering.

What body hair do you remove?

R: Nasal. When I reached 40, I started noticing those adverts in magazines for nasal trimmers. I trim every two–three weeks.

J: If I see some sticking out, I poke it back in!

What's your middle name?

J: Anne, after my mother.

R: Holt. It was also my father's middle name. It comes from a 19th century Madeley marriage involving a woman named Holt. Her name was added to ours as an honorary surname and it's been the middle name on the man's side ever since.

Who was the last person to tell you off?

R: Judy!

J: Richard got to the studio late because he'd gone to Selfridges to buy a birthday present.

R: I daren't tell Judy off!

J: You're always telling me off!

R: Actually, I did last night. When I got home Judy was in bed – and I like a smile when I get in, a little "hello, darling" – but I didn't get anything…

J: It was very hot and I was nearly asleep.

How often do you change your bed sheets?

R: Once a week.

J: The sheets are nice – white, one hundred per cent cotton.

What pants are you wearing?

J: Just standard black Lycra bikini briefs from M&S. They're very comfortable.

R: I haven't worn underpants for about ten years. They're restricting, you get hot… No, I don't get any chafing, just a little natural lubrication.

What does your best friend do for a job?

J: They're all in this business.

R: Two of our good friends, John and Emma, are actors. Our other friend, Russ, is our agent.

Tongues in public. Discuss.

J: We're getting a bit long in the tooth to worry about that kind of thing. I remember when we used to kiss in front of our kids and they'd be like, "Euuuurgh!"

R: If you're asking us if we'd do a little "tonsil tonguing" in public, though, probably not.

NICKY JOHNSTON

"I don't wear pants, but there's no chafing"
Richard

the Ultim... BIG BROT...

ARE YOU *BB*'S NO 1 FAN? THIS QUIZ WILL REALLY PUT YOUR KNOWLEDGE TO THE TEST

BIG BROTHER 1

Q1: What name did Darren give his favourite chicken?
- A: Marjorie
- B: Melanie
- C: Mary ✓

Q2: Who plucked her pubes with tweezers in the garden?
- A: Nichola
- B: Caroline ✗
- C: Melanie

Q3: What's the name of the housemate who won 41 per cent of the votes to come second?
- A: Anna ✗
- B: Craig
- C: Tom

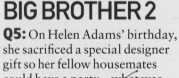

BIG BROTHER 2

Q4: Which two female housemates became more than friends, and ended up making headlines when they started dating a few months after the show finished?
- A: Anna and Melanie
- B: Sada and Nichola
- C: Nichola and Caroline ✗

Q5: On Helen Adams' birthday, she sacrificed a special designer gift so her fellow housemates could have a party – what was the present?
- A: A Prada dress
- B: A pair of Gucci shoes ✓
- C: Versace sunglasses

Q6: Who entered the house as a "surprise" after Penny was voted out?
- A: Stuart ✓
- B: Paul
- C: Josh

Q7: Which lovebirds kept talking about doing "stuff"?
- A: Elizabeth and Dean
- B: Helen and Paul ✓
- C: Brian and Josh

Q8: What is the name of the fun-loving hat wearer evicted in Week Five?
- A: Bubble ✓
- B: Rubble
- C: Stubble

BIG BROTHER 3

Q9: What was the "minging" thing that Jade and Adele had an argument about?
- A: Jade showing her Lulu
- B: A verruca on Jade's foot ✓
- C: A wart on her finger

Q10: What was the name of the saucy game that Kate and Alex played under the duvet?
- A: Follow the van ✗
- B: Dump the truck
- C: Lose the lorry

Q11: Which housemate did so badly in a house drinking game that she ended up completely naked?
- A: Kate
- B: Jade ✗
- C: Sophie

Q12: What's the name of the kilt-wearing housemate who escaped over the roof (not before weeing in the kitchen bin)?
- A: Sandy
- B: Adele
- C: Lynne ✓

BIG BROTHER 4

Q13: Which endearingly geeky housemate reckoned he had an invention for the "best toaster ever"?
- A: Cameron
- B: Ray
- C: Jon Tickle ✓

Q14: During his stay, Scots fisherman Cameron was picked to do a week's swap with a housemate from a different country. Where was the *Big Brother* house he visited?
- A: France
- B: Africa ✓
- C: Australia

nate quiz
HER

Q15: Which housemate had a penchant for make-up and went a bit overboard on the blusher?
- **A: Tania** ✔
- **B: Anouska**
- **C: Steph**

Q16: There was a "will-they-won't-they?" (they didn't, the spoilsports) romance between two of the *BB4* housemates – who were the twosome?
- **A: Nush and Scott** ✗
- **B: Steph and Ray**
- **C: Jon and Justine**

BIG BROTHER 5

Q17: What was the feathery nickname Michelle used for the object of her desire, Stu (and most other people for that matter)?
- **A: Duck** ✔
- **B: Chicken**
- **C: Goose**

Q18: What was the name of the all-male gang formed by Jason and Victor?
- **A: The Top Cats**
- **B: The Tigers**
- **C: The Jungle Cats** ✔

Q19: Which housemates were sent to live in a secret bedsit in order to spy on the house?
- **A: Emma and Michelle** ✔
- **B: Ahmed and Nadia**
- **C: Dan and Jason**

Q20: What cherished possession of Stuart's did evil BB set fire to?
- **A: His superhero cape**
- **B: His cowboy shirt**
- **C: His cowboy hat** ✔

Q21: What secret was Nadia hiding from her housemates?
- **A: She used to be a man** ✔
- **B: She was Portuguese**
- **C: She couldn't spell "balloon"**

BIG BROTHER 6

Q22: Which housemate thought she was pregnant?
- **A: Makosi** ✔
- **B: Sam**
- **C: Vanessa**

Q23: Who did Craig develop a major crush on?
- **A: Science**
- **B: Anthony** ✔
- **C: Maxwell**

Q24: What object Kinga "get to know" one night in the garden?
- **A: A hose**
- **B: A beer bottle** ✗
- **C: A wine bottle**

Q25: As the 2,000th housemate to enter the *Big Brother* Diary Room, what did Anthony win?
- **A: A week's supply of loo roll**
- **B: A date with Big Brother** ✔
- **C: A lap dance from Sam**

BIG BROTHER 7

Q26: What did Nikki refuse to drink in Week One?
- **A: Tap water** ✔
- **B: Bottled water**
- **C: Fizzy water**

Q27: What outfit did super-patriotic Welshman Glyn make his grand entrance to the house in?
- **A: A leotard**
- **B: A *Baywatch* costume** ✔
- **C: A Superman suit**

Q28: What was the nickname that Richard gave to the group formed by Sezer, Grace, Imogen and Mikey?
- **A: The Lipgloss Bitches** ✔
- **B: Plastic Fantastic**
- **C: The Plastics**

Q29: What did Grace hear the crowd chanting on the night that the Golden Ticket winner was chosen?
- **A: "Grace is a bitch!"**
- **B: "We hate Grace!"** ✗
- **C: "Get Grace out!"**

Q30: Which two housemates did Susie, the Golden Ticket winner, choose to face the public vote in her first week?
- **A: Grace and Imogen** ✔
- **B: Grace and Mikey**
- **C: Grace and Nikki**

How did you do?
Find the answers on **page 125**

'TIS THE SEASON TO BE MERRY...

When it comes to partying and letting their hair down, it seems stars are no different to the rest of us when it comes to having one too many. Alka-Seltza anyone?

JUNE BROWN

What have we here? Either June's feeling faint, or she's been at the festive sherry stash

HIC!

KIEFER SUTHERLAND

Oh, dear God. We hope Keifer isn't so hammered he's mistaken his seat for the toilet...

COLEEN McLOUGHLIN

"Tell Wayne I want a toasted kebab sandwich waiting when I get home"

MARTINE McCUTCHEON

Oh Martine, love! Being sick out of a car window is a bit teenage. You'd never catch Posh doing this

KINGA

No matter how much champagne she drinks, Kinga still remains the epitome of elegance

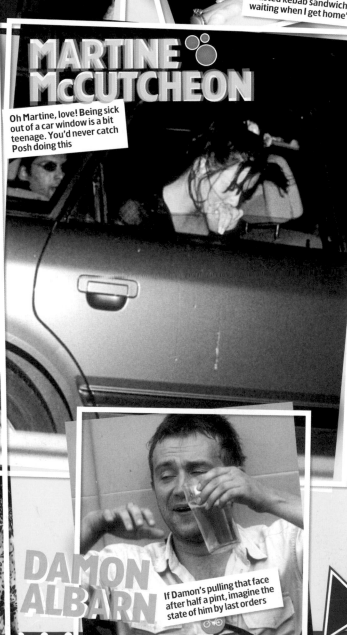

DAMON ALBARN

If Damon's pulling that face after half a pint, imagine the state of him by last orders

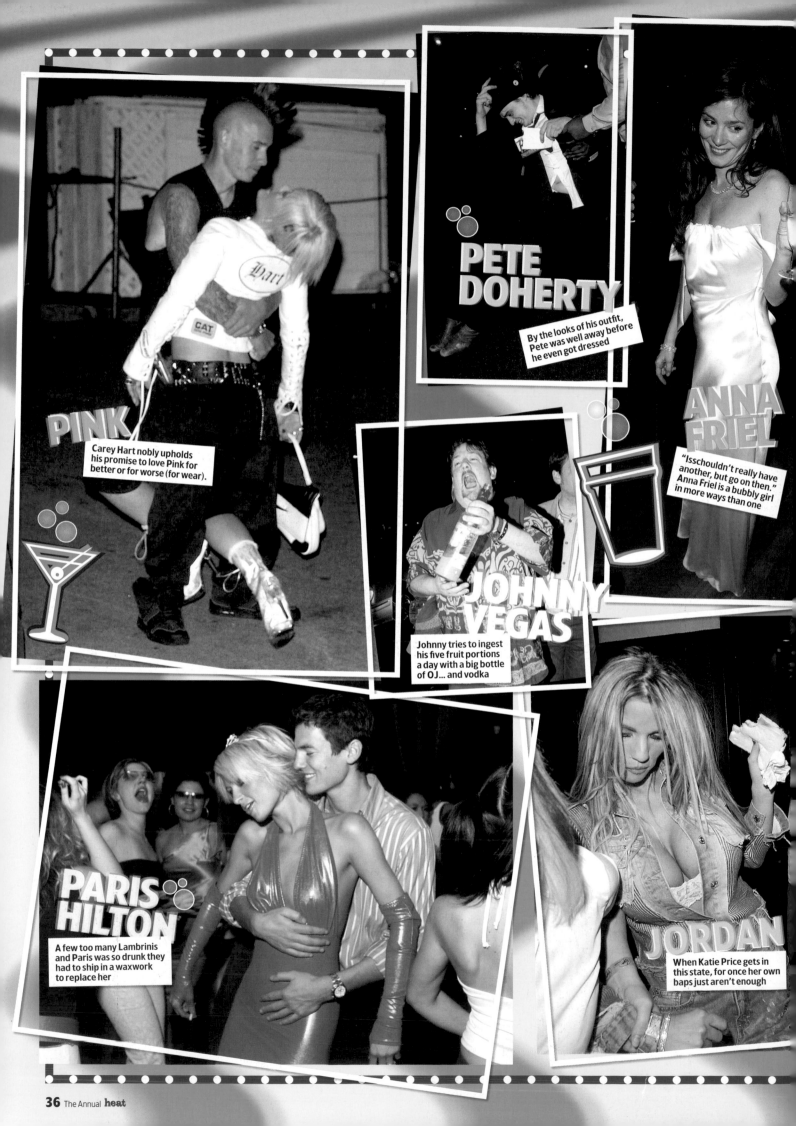

PINK

Carey Hart nobly upholds his promise to love Pink for better or for worse (for wear).

PETE DOHERTY

By the looks of his outfit, Pete was well away before he even got dressed

ANNA FRIEL

"Isschouldn't really have another, but go on then." Anna Friel is a bubbly girl in more ways than one

JOHNNY VEGAS

Johnny tries to ingest his five fruit portions a day with a big bottle of OJ... and vodka

PARIS HILTON

A few too many Lambrinis and Paris was so drunk they had to ship in a waxwork to replace her

JORDAN

When Katie Price gets in this state, for once her own baps just aren't enough

HIC!

MATTHEW McCONAUGHEY

Matt suffers from what's known as a bad case of Babycham legs and crashes out

NOEL GALLAGHER

Wahey! Who said Noel was a miserable, dour old git? It's amazing what a few shandies can do

TARA REID

When Tara said she was taking to the floor, we assumed she meant the *dancefloor*

JESSICA SIMPSON

Someone take that phone off her... Late night calls to exes are never a good idea, Jess

GEORGE CLOONEY

He looks happy, doesn't he? Might not be feeling so chipper in the morning tho'

PAMELA ANDERSON

As you can see, Pamela's wedding to Kid Rock was a low-key, sober affair

HIC!

CHARLOTTE CHURCH

Charl says she's cut down her drinking... to 15 pints a night?

GIRLS ALOUD

Moments later, Cheryl was flat out on the pavement, shouting for a dodgy burger

P DIDDY

He's famous for changing his name, so maybe we should start calling him P Squiffy

JUSTIN TIMBERLAKE

Any more of that potent-looking green stuff and Justin could be showing us his trousersnake

TINA O'BRIEN

One too many in The Rovers? Boyfriend Ryan Thomas gives Tina a hand

"There are certain advantages to doing intense workouts…"

January Brad Pitt

"I'm accustomed to taking my shirt off. I want to look my best, so I work out five times a week"

February
Jesse Metcalfe

March

David Beckham

"I don't feel embarrassed being called a sex symbol. It's flattering"

"I started working on my abs a long time ago. Hard work does pay off"

April Usher

"At first I went to the gym because I wanted to tone up, but now I have the bug"

May Philip Olivier

TOP TORSOS 2007

June
Justin Timberlake

"If people think I'm sexy, that's fine by me"

TOP TORSOS 2007

"I look at myself in the mirror – I need to see I look good"

July

Gavin Henson

TOP TORSOS 2007

August **Daniel Craig**

"I'd do a full frontal I'm not shy"

"I have a gym in my house – I'm into my health"

September
Eminem

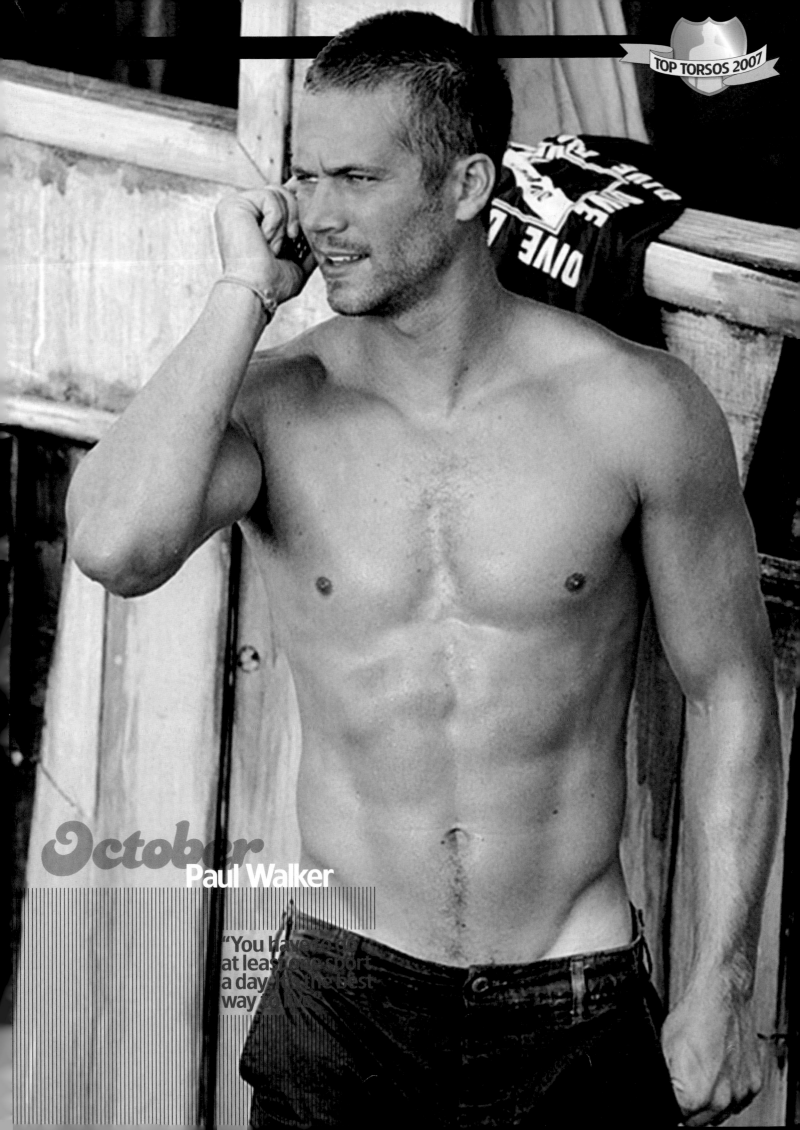

October
Paul Walker

"You have to do
at least one sport
a day — it's the best
way to..."

November
Matthew McConaughey

"I try to break a sweat every day, whether it's from running or swimming"

"I got a bit porky, so I've been going down the gym..."

December
Steve Jones

Calvin Klein

SIENNA MILLER
"I have a group of Bohemian friends. We get drunk and read from poetry books. It's one of my favourite things"

ANGELINA JOLIE
"I'm one of those people who needs to learn to let somebody hug me"

ACTOR CHAD MICHAEL MURRAY, ON HIS FIANCÉE KENZIE DALTON
"Imagine you are walking along and you trip over something. You turn around and find that it is a huge diamond. You would pick it up and do everything in your power to take care of that diamond, because it might take care of you for the rest of your life"

JENNIFER LOPEZ
"The bear is what we all wrestle with. Everybody has their bear in life. It's about conquering that bear and letting him go"

BRITNEY SPEARS
"I no longer practise Kabbalah. My baby is my religion"

GERI HALLIWELL
"I feel I am all things to all women"

MIKE SKINNER (THE STREETS)
"Trashing a hotel room is purer art than anything I've recorded. Consciously or unconsciously, I am creating art to sell it"

ASHTON KUTCHER, ON WIFE DEMI MOORE
"I hope the love we share can resonate around the world, so someday I can hear its echo"

'Oh, get o your

We know they're a world apart, but why stars ins

REESE WITHERSPOON
"I'm trying to matter, and live a good life and make work that means something to someone"

MADONNA
"I am my own experiment. I am my own work of art"

P DIDDY
"I feel safe in white because, deep down inside, I'm an angel"

EVA LONGORIA
"When I was a small child, people used to call me 'prieta fea' which means 'ugly dark one'. If I have a strong personality, it was because of being ugly when I was young"

OPRAH WINFREY
"I really believe that when you invite people to your home, you invite them to yourself"

DREW BARRYMORE
"I pray to be like the ocean, with soft currents, maybe waves at times. More and more I want the consistency, rather than the highs and the lows"

"It was finally time to take ownership of my body. I was blossoming now with body and soul"

TOBEY MAGUIRE
"I believe in a higher force that is within me"

MICHAEL JACKSON
"I see God in the face of children. If there were no children on this earth, somebody announced that all kids are dead, I would jump off the balcony immediately"

CHRISTINA AGUILERA
"I see myself as an ocean, because I'm really deep. And if you search deep enough, you can find rare, exotic treasures"

MATT LeBLANC
"I find the earth to be a place of misery in which I am surrounded by the conformity that kills society"

ver self!"

...ne

...speaking such pretentious waffle?

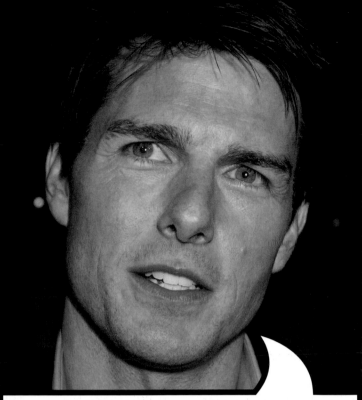

TOM CRUISE, ON THE BIRTH OF DAUGHTER

"It was spiritual. It was powerful. It was indescribable. It's still something that I'm processing and keep reliving"

NICOLAS CAGE
"My emotions are very close to my surface. I don't want to hold anything in, so it festers and turns into pus – a pustule of emotion that explodes into a festering cesspool of depression"

MAGGIE GYLLENHAAL
"I have a couple of girlfriends who are like, healing. We take care of each other. They know when I need to be taken care of"

ALICIA SILVERSTONE
"*Clueless* was very deep. It was deep in the way that it was very light. I think lightness has to come from a very deep place if it's true lightness"

JULIA ROBERTS
"Normally I have a great lightness of being. I take things in a very happy, amused way"

DANIEL DAY-LEWIS
"I've only been reminded in the last few days constantly that I've let five years pass. I'm not being deliberately obtuse about it, but I wasn't aware of that time passing"

BILLY BOB THORNTON
"I believe in running through the rain, crashing into the person you love and having your lips bleed on each other"

DENZEL WASHINGTON
"I made a commitment to completely cut out anything that might hamper me from getting my mind and body together. And the floodgates of goodness have opened upon me"

ELIJAH WOOD
"There is nothing noble in being superior to others. True nobility lies in being superior to your former self"

JENNIFER ANISTON

"I feel inwardly beautiful when I'm with my girlfriends and we are having a 'goddess circle'"

CELINE DION

"My child was not only carried by me, but by the universe"

stars 200

style

YOUR **22-PAGE** GUIDE TO LOOKING FABULOUS!

party dr

PEAR

Pear-shaped **J-Lo** doesn't agree with hiding her most famous feature. Celebrate curvaceous behinds with figure–hugging dresses that cinch in at the waist and broaden small shoulders to balance bigger hips.

Black and nude, Ariella @ House Of Fraser, £120; Navy with red bow, H&M, £39.99; Black ruched V-neck, Warehouse, £40

esses *to suit your shape*

CKS OUT SOME FABULOUS FROCKS

TUBE

Like **Cameron**, avoid structured, curvy-cut dresses as your figure will struggle to fill them. Instead, show off your lean physique with details and ruffles that create an illusion of curves. Choose a short length to avoid the walking-column effect.

lack belted,
ra, £39;
eam tunic,
&M, £29.99;
ft purple
ffle, French
nnection,
10

APPLE

Jade knows to go for an empire-line dress that accentuates the bust and covers up less-than-toned tums. For a flattering look, break it up with some kind of detail around your middle or a sash-belt around your waist.

Green halter-neck, Warehouse, £80; Red and cream, Monsoon, £110; Red and black strapless chiffon, Zara, £79

Like **Kelly**, flaunt your figure to the max in a dress that will nip in your waist and accentuate your womanly curves. Balance both your boobs and bottom with equal detailing and a pulled-in waist.

ack with roses,
w Look, £35;
arzipan yellow
iffon, French
nnection,
20; Pale pink
th black sash,
arehouse, £150

⭐ **STOCKISTS ON PAGE 125**

evening essentials

YOU'VE GOT THE DRESS, NOW ACCESSORISE YOURSELF TO STEAL THE SHOW

Cammina @
Sniff, £119.99

French Connection, £50

Butler & Wilson @
www.treasurebox.co.uk, £58

Accessorize, £25

Kleshna @ www.treasurebox.co.uk, £40.50

Butler & Wilson @ www.treasurebox.co.uk, £48

Accessorize, £40

Diva @ Miss Selfridge, £6

Accessorize, £40

Accessorize, £28

Russell & Bromley, £115

STOCKISTS ON PAGE 125

The Nosey Parker Interview

Abi Titmuss

Where are you now and what are you doing?

I am sitting in my living room, which is on the first floor. I live in a lovely town house that has a big floor-to-ceiling window and a plasma screen attached to the wall. I've just bought all these new plants as well. I decided that, as I don't have patients any more, I need something to care for. [Laughs.] I'm useless, though – they'll probably die in about a week.

What are you like in a strop?

You'll know about it. I'm not one of those people who can hide it; I wear my heart on my sleeve. I'm either happy or sad. I don't really sulk because I can't keep things inside.

How much do you weigh?

Less than Fern Britton and more than Victoria Beckham. [Giggles.] I'm training really hard at the moment and keep losing more weight every day. I can't say how much because it keeps changing.

Where's the weirdest place you've ever had sex?

I've had someone on various modes of transport: on a train, in the back of a black cab. The cab was the better, because even though I was in the first-class loo of the train, it wasn't very pretty!

What was the last call you avoided?

From one of my ex-bodyguards. I was supposed to meet him for lunch and I was running late. I thought, "I have to put it off for a day." I felt bad, though.

What body hair do you remove?

All of it, apart from a tiny bit in a certain place. Blokes should remove their hair, as well. They should do their balls, too – it's just so much nicer.

What's your middle name?

Evelyn. It's my grandma's name. With a name like Abigail Evelyn I used to get teased for being posh, when I'm not. When I was at primary school, *He-Man* was on the telly and there was a character in it called "Evil-Lyn". So the kids used to go to me, "Evil-Lyn, where's your staff?" I hated it.

Who was the last person to tell you off?

One of Prince Harry's tank commanders. He's a friend of mine and sent me a parcel recently to make me laugh – Dorset Nob biscuits. Have you seen them? He sent them to my manager's office and I kept not being arsed to go and pick them up. He got really annoyed and said, "Look, boys don't do post. I've made a huge effort, you could at least go and pick it up."

How often do you change your bed sheets?

The cleaner changes them every Friday. I love having someone else change the bed. When I was a nurse I changed beds for all those years. I'm talking 20, 30 beds, every day.

What pants are you wearing?

Some frilly little shorts from Victoria's Secret in Los Angele[s]. They've got a red and pink flower pattern on them.

What does your best mate do for a job?

I have three best mates and they all have great jobs. Two of them are in the music business. One of them works for the Rolling Stones, which is great because she gets to go all over the world. And there's another one who work[s] for Faithless. The third one works in PR.

Tongues in public. Discuss.

There's nothing worse – it's jus[t] a bit tacky isn't it? I don't thin[k] I've ever done it…

"I've had sex in the back of a black cab!"

it's in

SHE'S THE HANDBAG QUEEN, SO WHAT A-LIST ESSENTIALS DOES **COLEEN** CARRY AROUND

Cheese & Onion crisps

"I've never been into snacking on chocolate, but I love crisps – especially this flavour"

Vaseline

"You can't beat Vaseline for touching up dry lips and skin"

Lucky charm

"Wayne and I both have lucky charms. They're gold medals my dad gave us and I always keep mine with me"

Pink iPod

"Wayne bought me an iPod last Christmas and went to loads of trouble to get it in my favourite colour. I'm not really into gadgets, but I couldn't live without my iPod and Blackberry"

the bag

Water
"I drink it all day. It helps keep me trim"

LG Chocolate phone
"It's a great phone – it's black, has a touch screen and is quite a sexy little number"

Johnson's 3 in 1 Wipes
"I can't live without these wipes. They're just so handy and leave my skin feeling lovely"

Johnson's
3in1 FACIAL CLEANSING WIPES
Gently cleanse, tone & remove make-up even waterproof mascara

FOR SKIN

QUALITY GUARANTEE

25
(190 x

YSL Touche Eclat
"My one make-up lifesaver is YSL Touche Eclat under my eyes"

Nars Blush
"I wear this rouge every day but I don't wear eye make-up unless I'm going out"

Paul Smith Women
"My favourite perfume at the moment. Wayne gave it to me and it comes in a lovely bottle"

Pout Plump
"This lipgloss is one of my daytime basics"

fashion must-haves 2007

LEOPARD PRINT

Go wild this winter with the return of animal print. Forget memories of Kat Slater, this little leopard has shed its slutty image and is the pussycat print to be seen in. Wear it bold and striking and, for best results, accessorise with black or brown.

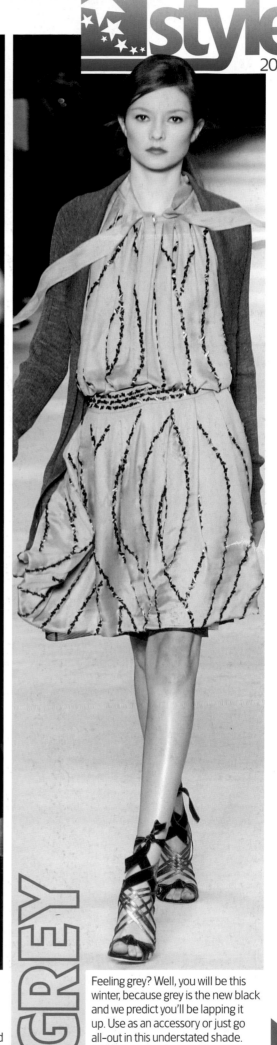

ANKLE BOOTS

The ankle boot, otherwise known as the shoeboot or pixie boot, is vital footwear for 2007. Worn with a skirt and cut-off tights, or with just a pair of skinny jeans, these boots are sure to punk up even the most classic of winter wardrobes.

JUMPER DRESS

There used to be nothing better than snuggling up in your favourite chunky knit, but the dawn of the jumper dress has taken cosy styling to another level. Wear with tights and ankle boots or over skinny jeans for the ultimate in comfortable chic.

GREY

Feeling grey? Well, you will be this winter, because grey is the new black and we predict you'll be lapping it up. Use as an accessory or just go all-out in this understated shade. Whatever your choice, this colour is super-stylish.

TARTAN

Prepare yourself for a Highland fling, because tartan's making a comeback this winter. The season will be all about Scottish style, so hit the high road and make it your fabric of choice for coats, skirts, trousers or hats. You'll look beautiful in big, bold checks.

BROCADE

Fashion is going back in time yet again with the return of brocade. Whether it's your coat, skirt or jacket, this rich, lavish fabric will give your look a vintage edge and have you looking and feeling high society in no time at all.

BAGGY TROUSERS

Baggy trousers are back. Mas... high-waisted pants have bee... a gorgeous girlie twist. Try we... them with a fitted shirt and a... of killer heels for some added... It's sure to put extra swagger... stylish step.

SHORT LENGTH

It's time to get those legs out, ladies: 2007 is all about the length and the length is short! Micro-mini dresses and flirty feminine coats are on the rise – as are their hemlines. Wear yours with thick tights or Lycra leggings to give you extra confidence.

BUBBLE SHAPE

The bubble has burst on the fashion scene in the form of billowing skirts, voluminous sleeves and puffball hems. The trick is to balance ballooning curves with tight-fitting tops. Team with heels to create a much-needed slimming effect.

LAYERS

Get ready to wrap up warm during the winter chill because layering will be hot. Try wearing a coat over a jumper dress over trousers – and don't forget your scarf and hat. The basic rule is that walking wardrobes are über-cool!

dear je

Spiders' legs

Dear Jemma,
When it comes to make-up, I feel more is more, but lately I've been having trouble seeing straight – could it be the blobs of mascara on my lashes? Pretty soon I won't be able to recognise Peter and who knows what that could lead to. How can I stop my lashes clumping together?

Jordan (34FF), Brighton

Dear Jordan,
I know you're a fan of the "bigger is better" idea but, when it comes to eyelashes, *less* is more. Clumpy mascara can be sexy – just got out of bed, bad-girl glamour – but save it for evenings and match it with smoky eyes and pale lipgloss.

For daytime, think subtle. Too much mascara and black eyeliner can make eyes look small and piggy – especially if your eyebrows aren't dark enough. Try a brown or clear mascara instead. Remove any excess with a tissue, then start at the root of the lash and stroke the mascara wand lightly upwards. For the lower lashes, use the end of the wand vertically, not horizontally, for more control. Not that you need more control, of course.
Love, Jemma

> Pout Wet Lash Clear Mascara, £16; Jemma Kidd Make Up School Lasting Tint, £12; YSL False Eyelash Effect Mascara, £18; Jemma Kidd Eyelash Curlers, £9

Circles of shame

Dear Jemma,
No matter what I do – well, maybe it's cos of what I do – I can't seem to shift the dark circles from under my eyes. Can you help?

Pete, no fixed abode

Dear Pete,
Heavy bags and dark circles under the eyes are a sign that something's not right. While you can cover them up, the only thing that will make them go away is clean living and plenty of sleep. Let's focus on covering them up, then. Black circles show through normal foundation, so you'll need a creamy concealer that blends well and soaks in. Dab a pink-toned concealer under the eye using your finger. Use a brush or sponge to work it right under the lash line and into the corner of the eye. Make sure the concealer is patted in and blend out at the edges. Powder isn't necessary. Then get some fresh air and eat some fruit.
Love, Jemma

> Jemma Kidd Make Up School Colour Match Concealer Duo in Fair, £11

mma...

I've been Tango'd

Dear Jemma,
Why am I so orange? All my teammates laugh at me; some of them even try to suck on me at half-time. It's not funny.
Gavin, Wales

Dear Gavin,
The Welsh sun isn't known for its strength and the secret of fake tan is to make people think it might just be real. This means it needs to tone in with your natural skin colour; fair skin goes apricot, then brown, *not* orange. Streaky or uneven tanning is also a fake-tan giveaway. To avoid this, prepare your skin first. Exfoliate thoroughly, moisturise all over and once it's absorbed, evenly apply a layer of fake tan. Wipes are a good way to start if you're not very experienced. Before you think about a second application, though, hold an orange up to your face and look in the mirror. If there is any similarity, step away from the bottle.
Love, Jemma

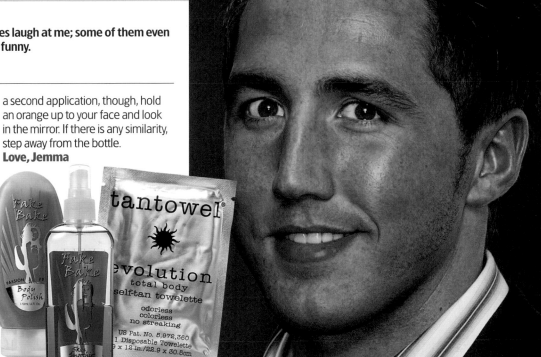

Fake Bake Passion Fruit Body Polish, £12; Fake Bake Skin Smoothie, £12; Tantowel Evolution Total Body Self-Tan Towelette, £2.49

Spot of bother

Dear Jemma,
People seem to think I'm still a fresh-faced youngster, which is fine by me, but my teenage-style spots are driving me mad. I get them all the time and they're, like, so gross. How can I cover and treat them?
Billie, central London

Dear Billie,
You should never squeeze spots. Instead, use a clay mask to draw out impurities. Always wash your make-up off at the end of the day and use antibacterial treatments with tea tree oil to stop them getting worse. You should think about chatting to a nutritionist about your diet as well. For coverage, look for a matt foundation that sinks into skin quickly and doesn't leave a powdery residue. For a raised spot, try dabbing on a creamy yellow-toned concealer and then leave it. Once it has dried, blend the edges around the spot into the skin for a natural look. To finish, dust your face with translucent powder, making sure you brush away any excess.
Love, Jemma

MAC Studio Touch Concealer, £11; Bourjois Matt Lovely Foundation, £6; The Body Shop Tea Tree Oil & Mint Daily Foaming Facial Wash, £5.50; Dr Hauschka Cleansing Clay Mask, £22

Loose lips

Dear Jemma,
What's a wealthy, buxom blonde to do if she likes to party but doesn't like her lipstick to smudge? Please help me!

Anna Nicole Smith, Hollywood

Dear Anna Nicole,
Life is hard. Older men tend to be bald and there's nothing like kissing a shiny pate to smudge your lipstick. Don't worry, though, help is at hand. Make sure your lips are smooth and well moisturised – try a beeswax-based balm, which will protect them. When the balm is fully absorbed, outline using a lipliner. I know you often wear red, but what with your blonde hair and thin lips, I suggest you try a neutral or pink liner instead. Pay attention to the bow of your lips, drawing slightly outside the natural line to make your top lip appear fuller. Fill in the whole lip area with the pencil, blending it with a brush, then try a pinky-beige lipstick on top. Put a dot of gloss in the centre of your bottom lip and press lips together. Gorgeous!
Love, Jemma

Burt's Bees Lip Balm, £2.99; Estée Lauder Pure Color Lipstick in Tiramisu; £14.50; Estée Lauder Artist's Lip Pencil in Pink Writer, £22.50

Red head

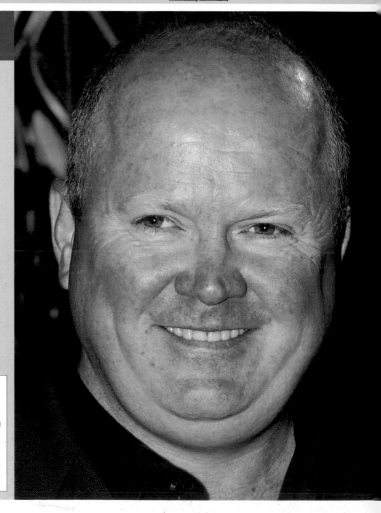

Dear Jemma,
I'm bright bleeding red with cheeks that glow like Rudolph's flaming nose. I've knocked the booze on the head so it can't be that. Do you think it's cos I've got an anger problem?

Phil Mitchell, Walford

Dear Phil,
Many things can lead to thread veins in the cheek, alcohol being one of them, so if you keep off the booze, you can still enjoy some shouting matches. Really severe veins can be treated at a clinic with laser treatment. The results are excellent, but it's not cheap. If you just suffer from high colour, you simply need to cover it with a good foundation. Red skin can often be dry and rough, so it's very important you moisturise well. Use a blob of creamy liquid foundation and gently pat it – not wipe it – into your skin. Let the foundation soak in and then blend at the edges so the colour looks even. Finish with a dusting of translucent powder.
Love, Jemma

Elemis Daily Redness Relief Moisturiser, £45; Chanel Vitalumière Satin Smoothing Fluid Makeup, £22; Chanel Natural Finish Pressed Translucent Powder, £22.50

No chips please

Dear Jemma,
I'm a busy girl with parties to go to, so it's totally annoying when my nail varnish chips after only a few days. How can I make it last?

Lindsay, Los Angeles

Dear Lindsay,
This is quite a tricky one, because once it's started chipping you need to whip it off. No ifs, no buts, young lady – just whip out the remover. Nail polish chips if your nails are ridged or uneven, so begin by buffing your nails with a four-sided buffer once a month. Next, soften cuticles in water or use a cuticle remover and then push your cuticles back gently. Make sure all traces

of oil are absorbed and then treat your nails with a base treatment. Then paint on two coats of your favourite nail varnish, making sure each coat dries properly before applying the next. Finish with a protective top-coat and you're done. This creates a high shine and lasts longer, chip free.
Love, Jemma

Barielle Ultra Speed Dry Manicure Extender, 12; Elegant Touch 4-Way Block Buffer, £2.25; Bliss Nail & Cuticle Super Groom, £12

Low brow

Dear Jemma,
I'm a 35-year-old woman and my fondness for a good pluck has left my eyebrows in a right state. Any tips?

Lea, Nottingham

Dear Lea,
A good plucking can be very satisfying, but it seems you've gone overboard. I am afraid there is only one thing to do – hide your tweezers in your bra and let those eyebrows grow back. Unfortunately, if you've been plucking for years, you may have damaged the hair follicle, which means the hair won't grow back and you'll have to continue drawing them on. The point is to make the drawn line look natural. Rather than a solid, black line, use a light-brown pencil or a stiff brush and brow powder. Instead of one line, use short, feathery strokes. These

look more like real hairs and create a far subtler result. I guarantee the permanently surprised look will be gone in seconds.
Love, Jemma

Estée Lauder Artist's Brow Mobile Essentials, £18; Benefit BrowZing Eyebrow Powder in Light, £21.50

★ STOCKISTS ON PAGE 125

The Nosey Parker Interview

Tara P-T

Where are you now and what are you doing?
I'm lying on my bed at home. I had a facial earlier. I've got an incredible lady from a skincare company called Darphin and she came to my house. It was so relaxing. I also did my usual hour-and-a-half piano practice this morning. I learnt to play the piano before I could walk and I've played at the Royal Albert Hall and The Festival Hall.

What are you like in a strop?
Pretty ugly, I "eff and blind" a lot. I've also thrown things before. I once had a row with a man in a hotel in Marrakesh and I threw my DVD player out of the window. Immediately afterwards I was like, "I wish I hadn't done that," because it was my prized possession. I only did it for effect and for full stroppy impact. It didn't even have the desired effect. The man just thought I was a spoilt little girl having a tantrum.

How much do you weigh?
Between 8st 3lbs and 8st 5lbs – I'd like to get a bit bigger. I would love to be 9st. Mainly in my boobs. I'd love a boob job, but I'm too much of a wimp to go through with it.

What was the last call you avoided?
It was from a reporter sniffing about. Why? Well, I would have thought that was obvious! Can't be arsed with all that.

Where's the weirdest place you've ever had sex?
Halfway down a mountain behind a tree when I was skiing. I was wearing a jacket and some tight little trousers, and I kept my skis on throughout. I wasn't worried about being seen by other people at all – that was half the thrill.

What body hair do you remove?
I have my eyebrows waxed and go for Brazilians, then I do my underarms and legs myself. But generally, I'm very hair-free.

What's your middle name?
Clare. There's no exciting reason behind it, but I wish it wasn't Clare because it meant that I was called TCP at school.

Who was the last person to tell you off?
My manager. He told me I need to grow up and not talk to journalists about private things unless I was prepared to pay the consequences. Sometimes things get taken out of context and I told someone – a journalist that I trusted – something private, and she printed it.

How often do you change your bed sheets?
Every other day. I've got a real thing about having clean sheets. They come from Frette, which is the finest sheet maker in the world. They're Egyptian cotton and they're the most nicey, pricey sheets ever. But I don't change them myself. I have an army of Russian maids for that.

What pants are you wearing?
None. I'm just wearing my Juicy Couture sweat pants. But I usually wear Cosabella pants. Britney Spears wears them, too. They're come in great colours. and are man-magnets.

What does your best mate do for a job?
I've got about five best friends. Phillip Treacy makes hats, Duncan James is a singer, Joe is a film producer, Carlos does my hair and make-up and Cleo Rochas is an actress.

Tongues in public. Discuss.
If I'm at a romantic landmark, I'm fine with it. But around friends, no chance. I think it's uncomfortable for other people to be around. I hate to see people going for it in the street.

"I'd love a boob job, but I'm too much of a wimp"

Shu Uemura Eyelash Curler, £18

This make-up artist fave will coax even the most stubborn lashes into open-eyed obedience. For maximum effect, curl three times, in stages, from root to tip. You'll never use another curler again.

Elizabeth Arden Eight Hour Cream, £19

Late nights and alcohol might do wonders for your social life, but they don't do your skin any good. The ultimate in facial first aid, this super-strength healing cream fixes dry patches and chapped lips. It also soothes sore, stressed-out skin in seconds.

Eight Hour
Cream
Skin Protectant
Crème de
Huit Heures
Baume Apaisant
Réparateur

12 beaut

GORGEOUSNESS GUARANTEED, NO MATTER WHAT YOU WERE UP TO LAST NIGHT

Kiehl's Creme de Corps, from £14

Covered up by winter layers, it's easy to forget our poor dehydrated bodies, but dry, dull skin isn't going to complement your party dress. For maximum moisture, copy Kate Moss and smother yourself in this amazingly nourishing cream.

Blistex, from £2.25

If too much kissing has left your lips a little worse for wear, then you'd better pop some Blistex in your bag. Angelina Jolie, owner of the world's most envied pout, uses it to keep her smackers sublime. Well, if it helped her bag Brad Pitt...

Bobbi Brown Shimmer Brick, £27

This shimmering powder – available in six beautiful shades – is the first stop for anyone wanting a natural-looking flush of colour. Five toning hues are blended together to create the perfect tool for giving you a gorgeous, hint-of-shine glow.

y things

you can't live without

A lesson in

She's famous for piling on the slap and gets through more lipliner than Pete Burns. Now, Jodie Marsh gives you a step-by-step guide to achieving her look. Trowels at the ready...

Step 1: **Preparation**

"Always start with last night's make-up on and old mascara halfway down your face. It's a good base to pile more on to and it's really good for your skin. Honest. Well, I don't have any spots."

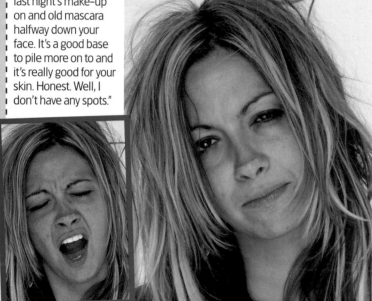

Step 2: **Foundation**

"It's best to go at least six shades darker than your natural skin tone. Slap on as much as possible and then go and stand in natural daylight, to check you have achieved a distinct tidemark."

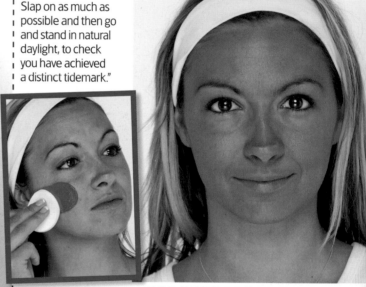

Step 5: **Bronzer**

"Choose a chocolate-brown colour and repeatedly apply it – ideally in a darkened room, so you can't tell how much you are using – it'll really stand out. A touch of glitter will help, too."

Step 6: **Lipliner**

"My trademark and favourite. Always use a blunt pencil and go at least a centimetre around your natural lipline for definition. Use the darkest shade you can lay your hands on. Or a black biro."

make-up...

Jodie Marsh xxxx

Step 3: Eyeshadow

"...st be black – think ...da eyes. Don't ...hy when it comes ...plication. Spread ... thick, circling the ...e eye. If bits fall ...our cheeks, don't ...ry: it will create ...ore dramatic look."

Step 4: Mascara

"Forget that 'replace your mascara every six months' rubbish. You want old really cloggy stuff – leaving it in the sun to dry out works well. Load onto lashes in several layers for a spidery–eyed look."

Step 7: Lipgloss

"...complement the ...er, I recommend ...lly pale colour. ...k Eminem's ex-wife ...e early days. Get ...e gloss on your ...h, men find it sexy ...n you lick it off in ...t of them."

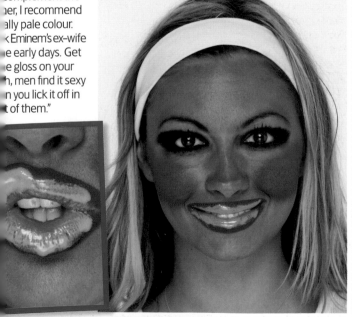

Step 8: Voila! It's time to party!

Spot the diff

A

ference

with David Letterman

How did you do?
Find the answers on **page 125**

The Nosey Parker Interview

Steve Jones

Where are you now and what are you doing?

I have absolutely no idea. I'm at a studio in London, but I was reading the paper coming up here. Where are we? I don't know if we're north, east, west or south. Where are we? Acton?

What are you like in a strop?

Terrible. I command perfection and if it doesn't go right, I am terrible. I don't get aggressive or nasty, or call anyone a twat, but I'm all exasperated and putting my head in my hands. It needs to be right. Everything. I'm actually getting in a strop now just thinking about it. [Laughs.]

How much do you weigh?

About 15st at the moment. It is all muscle now, but I put some weight on a few months ago when I quit smoking. Which was fucking hard by the way. But I'm a bit of a gym freak now. If I don't work out for a few days I get a bit twitchy.

Where's the weirdest place you've ever had sex?

The disabled toilets at Darling Harbour in Sydney. Was it when I went last Christmas? No, but it felt like Christmas.

What was the last call you avoided?

A second ago because a) it was from a withheld number and b) I'm talking to you. I don't like answering my phone when I'm with people.

What body hair do you remove?

Luckily, I've got a hair-free back. I have a bit of a hairy chest, but I don't do anything with that. I give my pubes a trim every now and again. My balls get a trim. It's a temple. I don't think girls want hairy balls in their mouths. Do they? Girls don't want a mound of hair. I'm the type of guy who washes his hands before he goes to the loo as well. Hygiene, baby. It's like

a new button "down there".

What's your middle name?

Ashton. Not as in Kutcher, I'm older than him. It was my grandfather's surname, they were the Ashtons.

Who was the last person to tell you off?

Richard Cook, my boss at *T4*. He was talking to the big boss at Channel 4 on the phone and I rushed into his office, going, "Cooky, so what's happening with this and that..." Basically, totally interrupting him. He said, "Two secs, Steve, please," but I carried on so he put me in my place. Actually, it was a lot less than that. He's going to read this and think, "What's he on about?" [Laughs.]

How often do change your bed sheets?

Quite regularly. Once a week. Sometimes more often when someone tips cranberry juice

all over them. Mentioning no names. It really pissed me off.

What pants are you wearing?

White Calvin Klein cotton boxers. I like the material they're made from. Actually, I quite like the band at the top.

What does your best mate do for a job?

He's a cameraman. Rob – he's my rock, my boy. I met him a few years ago and we lived together for a while. He's a good man. If I have problems, Rob's the guy I go to.

Tongues in public. Discuss.

Do it. Why not? It's your tongue. Use it. OK, use a bit of decorum, it's a bit much on the tube at rush hour and I've got Audrey and Philip necking down my ear. But if you're out and you're in a club somewhere, and it's like, 10pm, or 8 o'clock or even 7 o'clock, get on with it. I have no problems with tongues in public...

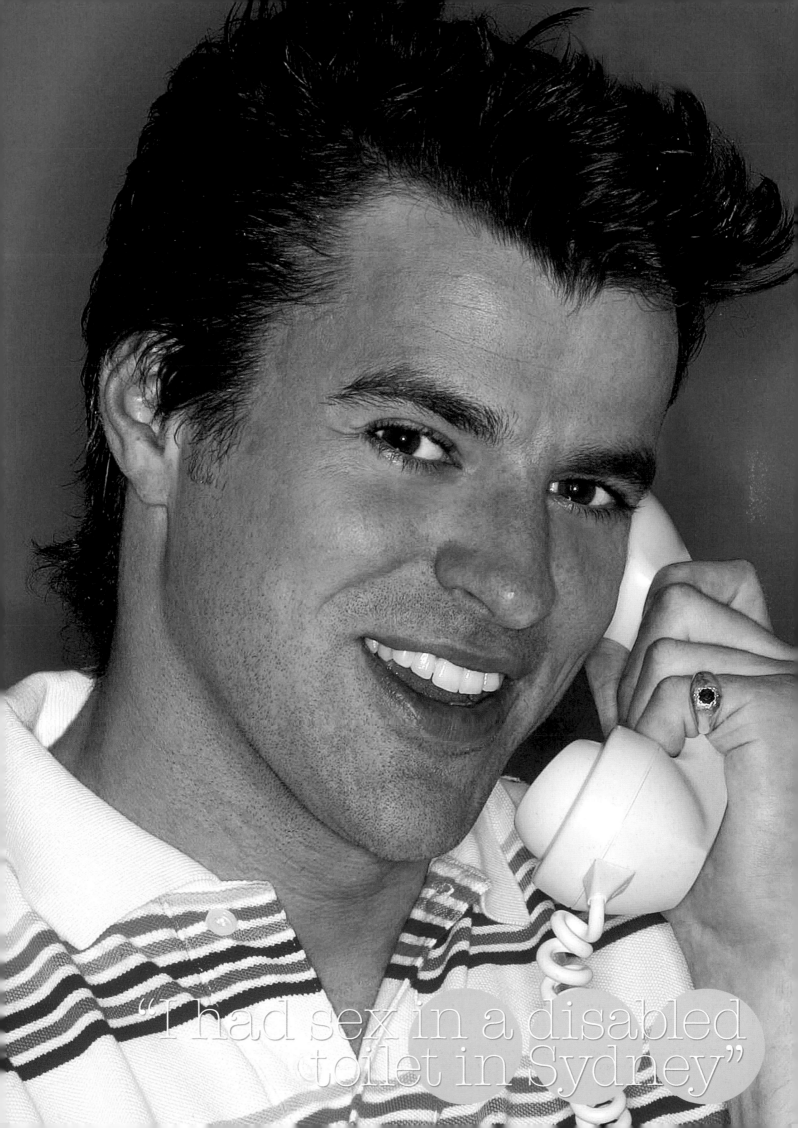

"I had sex in a disabled toilet in Sydney"

3rd

Robbie
Williams
WET PIT

Jessica
Simpson
ODD NORK

Teri
Hatcher
GIANT SHOE

**TURN OVER
FOR THE HIGHLY
COMMENDED**

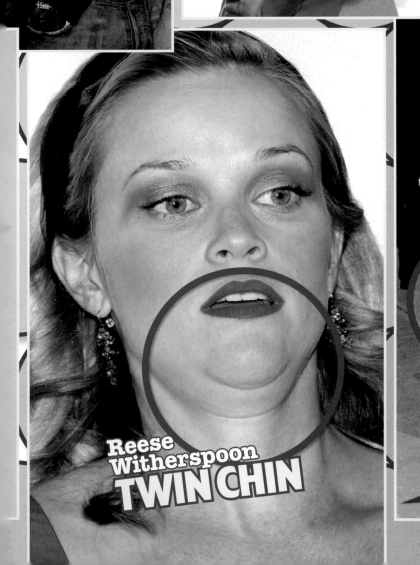

Reese
Witherspoon
TWIN CHIN

THE
Circle shame!
AWARDS 2007

HIGHLY COMMENDED • HIGHLY COMMENDED • HIGHLY COMMENDED • HIGHLY COMMENDED • HIGHLY COMMENDED • HIGHLY COMMENDED • HIGHLY COMMENDED • HIGHLY COMMENDED

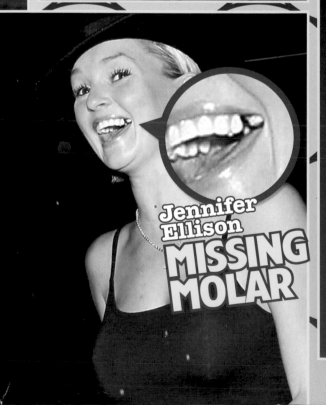

Tess Daly
FLUORO PANTS

Michelle Dewberry
TANGO ANKLES

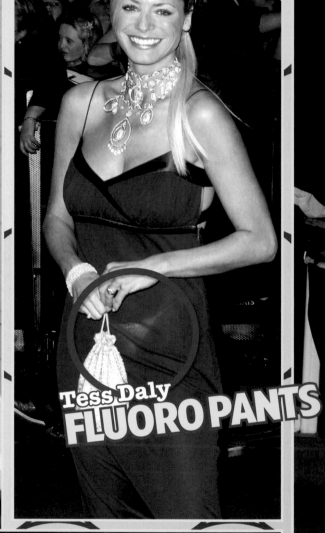

Jennifer Ellison
MISSING MOLAR

Jessie Wallace
CRACK ATTACK

Victoria Silvstedt
GRANNY GUSSET

TURN OVER FOR THE WINNERS

Lucy Davis
GHOST FACE

Serena Williams
COIN SLOT

LINDSAY LOHAN

KIEFER SUTHERLAND

KATE BECKINSALE

GOBBLE?

KIRSTIE ALLEY

MARTINE McCUTCHEON

PRINCE HARRY

GORGE!

THE A Z OF Paris Hilton

WHAT MAKES THE WORLD'S MOST FAMOUS HEIRESS TICK? TIME TO FIND OUT...

A for **ANCESTORS**
Paris is the all-American girl now, but her family tree is actually rooted in Europe. Her great-great-grandfather Augustus Halvorson Hilton was born on the family farm outside Oslo, Norway, before he emigrated to the US with his family.

B for **BOYFRIENDS**
The heiress' high-profile exes include Leonardo DiCaprio, Brandon Davis, Nick Carter, Jared Leto and Paris Latsis.

C for **CONNECTIONS**
Paris' great uncle Nicky was legendary movie star Elizabeth Taylor's first husband.

FIGHTS
Paris has had several high-profile girly bust-ups

D for **DOSH**
Last year, Paris' jewellery line, two perfumes, movie career, TV career and book royalties made her around $10million. She earns $300,000 for just turning up to a club.

E for **EXTRA WORK**
Aged one, Paris starred as Girl On The Beach in a TV movie called *Wishman*.

F for **FIGHTS**
So far, she's fallen out with Nicole Richie (who she's known since she was three years old!), Lindsay Lohan, Mary-Kate Olsen and Shannen Doherty.

G for **GHOSTS**
Paris reckons there's one at her grandparents' house. "A little girl who got run over in the driveway over 100 years ago. I've seen her in the mirror," she says.

H for **HAIR**
Left to its own devices, Paris's barnet would fizz up like a bottle of Coke after a long journey. "I have curly hair,' she admits. "I'd look like Shirley Temple if I didn't blow-dry it properly."

I for **INHERITANCE**
Paris' great-grandad Conrad left all his money to charities and the Catholic Church when he died Luckily for Ms Hilton, his son contested his will and won, meaning Paris and sister Nicky are heiresses to a multimillion dollar fortune.

J for **JUICY COUTURE**
"I always wear the tracksuits when I'm at home," says Paris. "But never wear gre ones – otherwise people think you might be working out."

DOSH
Paris can earn up to $10million a year

JUICY COUTURE
One of Paris' fave labels – although grey's a no-no

ZOO
Paris with kinkajou Baby Luv, a South American tree-dwelling mammal (!)

NICKY
Paris and her sister often go partying together

won't use any old product – she only likes Mystic Tan.

U for UNDERWEAR
Paris caused a big stink recently, when she took one of her pets, Baby Luv (see left), along with her to swanky lingerie shop Agent Provocateur and it bit and scratched her face.

V for VITAMIN WATER
The LA health drink is the secret to Paris' amazing partying stamina. "I hate champagne because it gives you hangovers," she says.

W for WEDDING
When Paris was first engaged to Paris Latsis, she wrote to Prince Charles asking him if they could be married in Westminster Abbey, St Paul's Cathedral or Windsor Castle.

X for X-RATED
Paris' infamous sex tape *1 Night In Paris* ended up in the hands of a distributor, who ended up selling 600,000 copies.

Y for YETI FEET
"I desperately hate one thing about my body," Paris says. "I have size 11 feet." That's a whopping size nine to us Brits.

Z for ZOO
Animal-crazy Paris has two Chihuahuas called Tinkerbell and Bambi, three Pomeranians, a ferret named Dolce & Gabbana, a bobcat, rats, snakes, cats and an iguana.

K for KATHY HILTON
Paris' mum was only 15 when she met Rick Hilton, and 19 when she had Paris.

L for LENSES
Paris naturally has brown/dark green eyes but she won't be seen dead in public without her blue contact lenses. Or a pet and mobile phone.

M for MIDDLE NAME
Introducing… Paris Whitney Hilton.

N for NICKY
Sister Nicky is three years younger than Paris. The pair are best friends and are often spied out on the town together. "When we were younger, I'd dress up as the Queen and make her be a princess," says Paris.

O for OPERATIONS
Paris's view on plastic surgery: "I don't need it and I would never get it. But maybe if I looked like some of those girls with really big noses I would." Diplomatic, as ever…

P for PUBLICIST
Paris' publicist is Elliot Mintz, who used to represent John Lennon and Yoko Ono.

Q for QUOTE
In October 2004, Paris had her favourite and famous phrase "That's Hot" trademarked, and is working on a clothing line of the same name.

R for RECORD LABEL
Paris set up Heiress Records in 2004, to release her own music.

S for SPORT
Paris has been playing ice hockey since she was 16. She lists her favourite sports as golf and "frog hunting on my ranch".

T for TANNING
She reportedly spends $15,000 a year on keeping her skin that perfect sunkissed shade. But Paris

The NOT-SO-BIG CROSSWORD

ACROSS

1 She left Doctor Who's side in July 2006 (6, 5)
6 Johnny Knoxville played this Duke in the *Dukes Of Hazzard* movie (4)
7 His best-selling novel was released as a Tom Hanks blockbuster (3, 5)
9 Brandon Routh donned the cape in *Superman* ------- (7)
11 Heist comedy starring Bruce Willis and Billy Bob Thornton (7)
12 Actress ---- Thompson plays Professor Trelawney in the Harry Potter movies (4)
14 *Hips Don't Lie*, reckons this Latino popstress (7)
15 Del Toro starred in *The Usual Suspects* and *Sin City* (7)
18 Big UK music awards that happen every year (4)
19 Gwyneth Paltrow opened these Doors (7)
21 Jonathan Ross' investigative wife, Jane ------- (7)
23 Nielsen was surprised by Jackie Stallone in last year's *Celeb BB* (8)
24 Hugh Grant and Julianne Moore spent these Months together in 1995 (4)
25 Royal butler turned Reality TV show buffoon (4, 7)

DOWN

1 Sid Owen is the latest edition to this TV prison series (3, 5)
2 Shane found himself marooned on *Love Island* (5)
3 As Bridget Jones, Renée Zellweger teeters on The ---- *Of Reason* (4)
4 Matt Damon sequel *The Bourne* ---------- (9)
5 Rula fed George Galloway milk on *Celebrity BB* (6)
8 He directed *Match Point*, starring Scarlett Johansson (5, 5)
8 She didn't win *The Apprentice* in 2006, but she sure did entertain us (4, 6)
10 Classic 1976 De Niro film also starring Jodie Foster ---- *Driver* (4)
13 Britney's little sis (5, 4)
16 This Moon kicked the bucket in *EastEnders* (4)
17 Noel's *Deal* -- -- ---- was a 2006 phenomenon (2, 2, 4)
18 Christian Bale starred in *Batman* ------ (6)
20 Holmes did her best to give birth quietly this year (5)
22 Jessica ----, star of *Fantastic Four* and *Sin City* (4)

(Crossword grid, partially filled in by hand:)

1 ACROSS: BILLIE PIPER
9 ACROSS: RETURNS
12 ACROSS: EMMA
14 ACROSS: SHAKIRA
25 ACROSS: PAUL BURRELL
23 DOWN/ACROSS: BRIGITT...

H	R	J	K	F	M	G	G	F	F	H	F	J	F	J	F	G	E	A
M	N	A	B	Y	L	N	E	E	R	G	R	E	V	E	R	D	F	Z
I	J	N	B	O	B	I	Y	V	C	O	D	F	C	S	R	D	S	E
C	K	Y	N	U	B	Y	G	U	I	O	M	J	D	Y	G	H	W	P
D	A	T	V	A	E	R	T	H	D	C	S	N	Y	H	W	S	I	O
L	X	H	X	N	E	D	C	F	T	A	I	A	O	N	B	V	T	A
I	A	I	E	D	W	W	S	E	D	M	W	S	V	W	G	B	C	H
H	B	N	B	I	C	O	S	X	S	V	Y	S	X	M	O	M	H	N
C	S	G	A	Q	E	D	D	B	U	J	K	F	A	D	C	N	I	M
S	F	I	B	V	N	M	O	E	K	L	Y	H	I	R	F	T	T	U
Y	F	S	Y	U	I	L	O	P	M	G	O	N	J	R	L	M	O	O
A	W	P	E	D	C	H	N	W	S	T	R	K	L	O	E	P	N	I
D	T	O	T	O	W	S	D	N	Y	H	E	M	A	G	R	U	O	Y
I	C	S	P	V	I	M	A	O	H	W	N	L	K	M	J	N	H	B
R	A	S	E	D	I	O	H	P	T	G	Q	A	T	H	J	W	S	I
F	B	I	B	L	E	A	V	E	R	I	G	H	T	N	O	W	T	G
S	X	B	Q	A	U	H	E	E	I	J	O	O	P	E	O	W	S	E
X	G	L	F	G	J	Y	U	K	P	O	K	G	F	W	S	D	V	V
Q	S	E	C	C	E	V	O	L	E	M	I	T	L	L	A	E	G	J

THE WILL YOUNG WORDSEARCH

- ☐ From Now On
- ☐ Friday's Child
- ☐ Keep On
- ☐ Anything Is Possible
- ☐ Evergreen
- ☐ Light My Fire
- ☐ Don't Let Me Down
- ☐ You And I
- ☐ Leave Right Now
- ☐ Your Game
- ☐ Switch It On
- ☐ All Time Love
- ☐ Who Am I
- **BONUS:**
- ☐ Roy

You know all his hits, but can you find them here?

How did you do?
Find the answers on **page 125**

fantasy spotted!

they can't get away from us!

- **Courtney Love** buying all-purpose stain remover from Asda in Liverpool
- **David Beckham** throwing a bottle of water over Victoria's head, after her hair extensions caught fire during a candlelit dinner at TGI Friday's in Romford, Essex
- **Jade Goody** engrossed in an advanced Sudoku puzzle in the first-class carriage of a train to Cambridge, East Angular
- **Britney Spears** emerging from a Beverly Hills health-food store, clutching a bag of mung beans, in a chic designer trouser suit and stilettos

- An incognito **Will Young** buying a *Valley Of The Busty Babes* DVD from Blockbuster in Gravesend, Kent

top spot!

Robbie Williams, Judy Finnigan, Liam Gallagher, Kerry Katona, Jackie Stallone and J-Lo all smeared in whipped cream, having an orgy on Nelson's Column in London's Trafalgar Square
LIZ WINDSOR, BUCKINGHAM PALACE

- **David Icke** offering up a goat for worship at a satanic meeting in Blackpool

- **Charlotte Church** flushing **Cheryl Tweedy**'s head down the loo after coming to blows during a speed-dating night in central London
- **Mischa Barton** looking dog rough in a grey boiler suit and chomping on a Pepperami on the top deck of a Megabus from Leeds to Glasgow
- A smiley **Mariah Carey** rushing to serve herself and her dining companions plates and cutlery at Nando's in Ipswich
- A loved-up **Nicole Kidman** and **Keith Urban** playing Poohsticks from a bridge over the River Freshney in Grimsby
- **Calum Best** telling a group of sulky teenagers how fulfilling abstinence is, at a True Love Waits meeting in Woking
- A dishevelled **Paris Hilton** rummaging through a basket of old cassette tapes in the Save The Children charity shop in Mansfield, Nottinghamshire
- **Gareth Gates** body-popping to Vanilla Ice while a gaggle of girls, including **Hayley Evetts**, looked on admiringly at Moseley Dance Centre in Birmingham
- A jovial **James Blunt** leading the guests with an impressive rendition of *Agadoo* at a community centre in Chatteris, Cambridgeshire
- **Keira Knightley** weeping on Morecambe seafront after failing to win the part of Widow Twankey in panto
- A delighted **Madonna** winning a Bacardi Breezer after coming third in a Madonna-themed karaoke comp at Pontin's in Prestatyn Sands, Wales
- **Angelina Jolie** getting some bling diamanté nail art applied during a manicure at a nail bar in Brixton, south London
- **Russell Brand** waiting in line at a dating agency in Dagenham behind **David Walliams**, who was telling the manager, "I'm painfully shy and just don't know how to meet women. Please help me"

TREVOR McDONALD and his morris-dancing troupe entertaining the crowds at The Royal Bath & West agricultural show

- **Jordan** and **Peter Andre** rushing across Brighton train station car park to warmly hug **Jodie Marsh** and **Javine**, who'd travelled down from London to see them
- A sweaty **Phillip Schofield** moshing at a Lordi gig, while a leather-clad **Fern Britton** crowd-surfed over his head at Fibbers in York
- **Teri Hatcher** tucking into bubble and squeak and wiping a stray fleck of egg yolk from **Dean Gaffney**'s lips, while gazing lovingly into his eyes at a greasy spoon in New Cross, London
- **Chris Martin** cramming a Happy Meal into Apple's mouth, while Gwyneth Paltrow asked for her Big Mac Meal to be supersized at McDonald's in Nantwich
- A dressed-down **Coleen McLoughlin** backpacking around Eastern Europe wearing grubby dungarees, hiking boots and no make-up

COLIN FARRELL somersaulting down a hillside after an 8lb Double Gloucester at the annual Cheese Rolling event at Cooper's Hill, Gloucestershire

PETE DOHERTY
well-groomed and clean-shaven, strutting down Bond Street, London, in a sharp suit, leaving a waft of expensive aftershave in his wake

MICHAEL DOUGLAS
hanging out with 15-year-olds, wearing a hoodie and throwing chips at passers-by in Swansea town centre

●A serene **Naomi Campbell** presenting her maid with an Employee Of The Month trophy and treating her to a Curry Club dinner at a Wetherspoon's pub in Mile End, east London
●A sweaty **Jennifer Aniston**, in PVC hotpants and a fluffy orange bra, clutching a glow stick while gyrating on a podium with a scantily clad **Michelle Bass** at Space in Ibiza
●A jovial **Michael Jackson** judging a wet T-shirt contest at Pulse nightclub in Stevenage

crap spot!

Some random bloke who was a runner-up on *Blockbusters* in 1988 walking down a street somewhere with no expression on his face
BEYONCE KNOWLES, GRIMSBY

●**Brad Pitt** chomping on a sticky red toffee apple and incurring the wrath of some teenagers after ramming them from behind on the dodgems at Great Yarmouth Pleasure Beach
●**Gisele Bündchen**, smelling of beef-flavoured Monster Munch, getting a backie from **Wayne Rooney** as he pedalled furiously through Toxteth, Liverpool, on a stolen BMX

DISCLAIMER: SOME OF THE SIGHTINGS MIGHT BE IN OUR HEAD. OK, ALL OF THEM ARE

●An animated **Lindsay Lohan** playing backgammon with mystery pensioner at an old folks' home in Jersey, but getting distracted by the *Bergerac* omnibus on UK Gold
●**Peaches** and **Fifi Geldof** comparing ringtones on their mobiles before indulging in a spot of happy-slapping at a bus stop outside Somerfield in Cricklewood, north London
●**The Banker** from *Deal Or No Deal* demanding of a snooty Soho maitre d', "Don't you know who I am?" before realising his mistake
●**Simon Cowell** buying some low-rise jeans and a baggy white T-shirt from Gap in Bluewater shopping centre, Kent
●**Matt Lucas** effortlessly swimming the Atlantic Ocean wearing a mermaid's tail and light-up deely-boppers
●A chirpy **Jude Law** playing hopscotch with a jolly paparazzi photographer on Primrose Hill
●The cast of **Desperate Housewives**, all wearing fairy wings, demonstrating their sexual techniques on empty Smirnoff Ice bottles during a girls' night out at Caesar's club in Streatham, south London

●**Louis Walsh**, head to toe in neon-pink Lycra, enthusiastically shaking his booty at a Legs, Bums & Tums class in Northampton
●**Justin Timberlake** going unnoticed as he smeared vegetable oil over his chest while wearing a zebra-print posing pouch on Southend seafront

●A giggling **Gillian McKeith** buying three packets of Pringles and some Hob Nobs while puffing on a suspicious-looking cigarette at a 24-hour garage in Lewisham, south east London
●**Hugh Grant**, in a Green Day hoodie, tearing up the half pipes at a skate park in Walsall

PRESTON & CHANTELLE
splashing around enthusiastically in the shallow end during an aquafit class at Trowbridge Sports Centre in Wiltshire

The Nosey Parker Interview

Vernon Kay

Where are you now and what are you doing?
I'm in the back garden at home, relaxing. I'm looking after my two-year-old, Phoebe, and our dog, Sam. Phoebe's just had shepherd's pie for dinner but she's wiped it all over her stomach and Sam's trying to lick it off!

What are you like in a strop?
I sulk. One thing that gets me is people dropping litter. Sometimes, when I've been sitting at traffic lights and people have done it out of their car windows, I've got out and said something! Losing things gets me in a strop, too. You know when you hide something in a secret place, then forget where it is? I'm always doing that with my car keys.

How much do you weigh?
About 12st. At 6ft it's OK, but I'm skinny. I went to the gym to bulk up, then I ate loads of lard, but nothing helped. I'm happy with my weight now. If tall and thin works for Peter Crouch, it can work for me!

Where's the weirdest place you've ever had sex?
I can't say! My mum will read it! Was it good? I'm smiling…

What was the last call you avoided?
One from my younger brother, Steven. He's always calling to borrow my clothes. I was just busy when he rang.

What body hair do you remove?
Nasal hair is a big faux pas. James Redmond got me noticing mine when I was 22. We were at a Verve gig in Wigan when he told me to "sort it out". I control it now with nasal trimmers. It makes breathing much easier.

What's your middle name?
Charles. There's no reason for it, but I'm Vernon after my dad's dad. I like my name now, although I used to want to be "Mark". Weirdly, there's a Vernon Street in Bolton where they used to put down stray cats and dogs. When I was born people were like, "Why have you named him after that?"

Who was the last person to tell you off?
My dad, Norman, told me off for taking the mickey out of him. He's a trucker so he doesn't get much exercise and I was taking the mick out of his pot belly and his one-arm tan. I mentioned his nasal hair, too.

How often do you change your bed sheets?
Every three weeks. Tess and I have great sheets – Frette Egyptian linen ones. We got four sets as a wedding present.

What pants are you wearing?
White Calvin Klein boxer shorts. I have loads, all in white. When I was filming in America Bloomingdale's had a sale so I bought a suitcase full. I couldn't be a thong man – me in a thong from behind would look like absolutely hideous because I'm so thin!

What does your best friend do for a job?
My best friend is Luke and he's a primary school teacher for 8 year-olds. We don't see each other much, but when we do we just go to the pub for a drink and a chat. He's usually with me when people come and ask to take my photo to get printed in *heat* for £20 or whatever!

Tongues in public. Discuss.
I don't mind seeing it as long as they're not slobbering. Once, Tess and I were photographed snogging while leaving Nobu. I remember seeing the photo in the papers and turning the page really quickly. Urgh!

ELLIS PARRIIDER

"Nasal hair is a big faux pas. I use trimmers"

ANT & DEC:

HOW MUCH DO YOU KNOW ABOUT TELEVISION'S FAVOURITE CHEEKY CHAPPIES?

Q1: Ant had a brief stint on which classic 70s kids' TV show?
- **A: *Why Don't You?***
- **B: *Cheggers Plays Pop***
- **C: *Multi-Coloured Swap Shop***

Q2: How many albums have the Geordie duo released?
- **A: Three**
- **B: Two**
- **C: One**

Q3: In photos and on telly, Ant is almost always on the left and Dec on the right. But according to a 2004 *Daily Mirror* poll, what percentage of people couldn't tell the cheeky pair apart?
- **A: 50 per cent**
- **B: 70 per cent**
- **C: 90 per cent**

Q4: Which former *Blue Peter* presenter did the duo describe as "up for it" live on air during the pre-watershed *Ant & Dec Show*?
- **A: Anthea Turner**
- **B: Katy Hill**
- **C: Janet Ellis**

Q5: In *Byker Grove*, how was Ant's character, PJ, blinded?
- **A: By staring at the sun during an eclipse**
- **B: When a camping gas canister exploded**
- **C: When a paintball hit him in the eye**

Q6: What was the name of their celeb-packed, spoof sitco on *SM:TV Live*?
- **A: Mates**
- **B: Pals**
- **C: Chums**

Q7: What year did Ant & Dec start presenting charity show *I'm A Celeb…*?
- **A: 2002**
- **B: 2003**
- **C: 2004**

Q8: On what did the boys splash out a whopping £175,000 in February 2003?
- **A: A luxury holiday in the Bahamas for both of their famili**
- **B: Half of their favourite Newcastle pub, Johnny Ringos**
- **C: Shares in Newcastle United**

Q9: How many siblings does Dec have?
- [ ] **A:** Six – three brothers and three sisters
- [ ] **B:** Three brothers and a sister
- [ ] **C:** One brother

Q10: Ant is taller than Dec, but by how much?
- [ ] **A:** Ant, at 5ft 9ins, is one inch taller than 5ft 8ins Dec
- [ ] **B:** Ant, at 5ft 11ins, is four inches taller than 5ft 7ins Dec
- [ ] **C:** Ant, at 5ft 8ins, is two inches taller than 5ft 6ins Dec.

Q11: Dec almost followed his brother, Dermot, into his profession. What was it?
- [ ] **A:** Primary school teacher
- [ ] **B:** Second-hand car salesman
- [ ] **C:** Priest

Q12: Which of the following is Dec afraid of?
- [ ] **A:** Pigeons
- [ ] **B:** Heights
- [ ] **C:** Cotton wool

Q13: What is Ant's pet hate?
- [ ] **A:** Rude waiters
- [ ] **B:** Soap operas
- [ ] **C:** Shaving rash

Q14: Ant & Dec are worth approximately how much?
- [ ] **A:** £5million
- [ ] **B:** £10million
- [ ] **C:** £20million

Q15: How old were the pair when they won a Special Recognition Award at the 2002 National Television Awards?
- [ ] **A:** 27
- [ ] **B:** 30
- [ ] **C:** 33

Q16: What size are Dec's feet?
- [ ] **A:** 6.5
- [ ] **B:** 8
- [ ] **C:** 10

Q17: Best friends for years, the pair have only ever had one fight. Where did the scuffle take place?
- [ ] **A:** Over a girl when they were 16. Ant floored Dec in a pub
- [ ] **B:** In a lift in Spain – Ant punched Dec in the chest and Dec knocked his cap off
- [ ] **C:** Over the remote when they were living together. Ant wanted to watch *Bullseye* and Dec wanted to watch *Antiques Roadshow*

Q18: Dec's dad has an unusual name – what is it?
- [ ] **A:** Evelyn
- [ ] **B:** Alphonsus
- [ ] **C:** Bacchus

Q19: Dec was a student at St Cuthbert's Catholic High School in Newcastle. Who are the other famous alumni?
- [ ] **A:** Sting and the Pet Shop Boys singer Neil Tennant
- [ ] **B:** *Big Brother*'s Johnny and radio DJ Lauren Laverne
- [ ] **C:** Jimmy Nail and Alan Shearer

Q20: To mark the 30th anniversary of The Prince's Trust, the boys conducted an exclusive interview with Princes Charles, William and Harry. What TV show did the royals admit to watching together?
- [ ] **A:** *EastEnders*
- [ ] **B:** *Friends*
- [ ] **C:** *The Bill*

How did you do?
Find the answers on **page 125**

Look into my eyes

heat's astrologer Hectic Smeg gives her amazing predictions* for the world of showbiz over the next 12 months

I see red people...

Britney Marries Michael Jackson

Fed up with Kevin going out to yoga classes every night, Britney takes up Jacko's offer of a trip to Neverland with her kids. Once there, they fall in love on his carousel and Brit sends Sean Preston back to Kev with a note saying she's leaving him for someone who really loves children.

Victoria Beckham Designs A Line For Evans

After listening to too many Elvis records, Posh gets hooked on his favourite deep-fried peanut butter sandwiches and puts on 16st in three days. She is approached by the plus-size clothing chain to design a pair of elasticated waistband trousers, which quickly become their top-selling item.

Peter Andre Runs For PM

After 18 months of marriage to Jordan, Pete goes in search of a less challenging role and runs for Prime Minister. His campaign song, a gospel/hip hop cover of *I've Got A Lovely Bunch Of Coconuts* tops the charts. Sadly, I don't see success for Peter. Instead, he'll become MP for Brighton, pushing for lower tax on imported fake tan.

Pamela Has A Breast Reduction

I *think* she does, anyway. I can't see through my psychic mist at the moment, but they definitely look smaller from where I'm standing. Hic.

Kate Moss Goes To Bed Early

It's true, I can feel it in my mystic waters. After 578 nights out on the trot not getting in before 8am, Kate stays in on a Monday night, rents loads of DVDs (including one about the 1978 Chelsea Flower Show) and needs to be put to bed by her daughter Lila at 7.59pm.

Coleen Gets Caught Shoplifting

Bored of paying for everything, I feel Coleen will try to steal a Rimmel eyeliner from Superdrug. But she'll be caught and will spend the rest of her life doing hard labour in prison. Oh well.

Angelina Pulls Jennifer

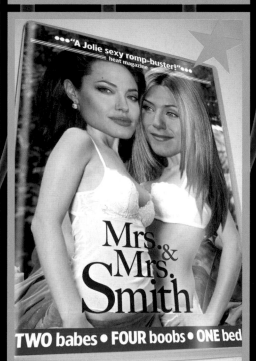

•••"A Jolie sexy romp-buster!"•••
heat magazine

Mrs. & Mrs. Smith

TWO babes • FOUR boobs • ONE bed

The ladies meet to put their ghosts to rest, but Ange realises she prefers Jen to Brad. As she's seducing her, Brad walks in, videos the whole thing on his cameraphone and makes it into a romantic comedy/drama which grosses $14.2billion at the US box office. They all go off to live a life of polygamy in Utah.

Jordan Goes To Oxford Uni...

...But only because she is giving a talk on inflatable dildos at the Union.

FREE benefit make-up set!

ONLY WHEN YOU SUBSCRIBE TO heat

WORTH £34

4 GREAT REASONS TO SUBSCRIBE

1 Free Benefit make-up worth £34
2 *Only £6.30 per month when you pay using easy direct-debit instalments
3 Hot gossip at a cool price!
4 FREE delivery direct to your door every week

CALL 0870 124 1080 (QUOTE GPCC)

HURRY
while stocks last!

or subscribe online at
www.greatmagazines.co.uk/annual

All the answers!

Spot The Difference — PIC B
PAGE 20

1 Flag on the tower above Mariah is flying in the opposite direction
2 Mickey's hat is a different colour
3 There is a tower missing from the trees to the right of Mickey
4 One of Mickey's eyes is closed
5 Mickey's waistcoat has a yellow button missing above his hands
6 Mariah's butterfly brooch is facing downwards
7 There is a button missing on the left-hand side of Mickey's trousers
8 The woman standing to the right of Mickey, near the two men by the tree, is missing
9 There is a ribbon missing from the back of Mariah's dress
10 Mariah's thin ankle bracelet is missing

Guess Who?
PAGE 24

BRIT SINGER Duncan James
FAMOUS DAUGHTER Kate Hudson
POSH BRIT ACTRESS Kate Beckinsale
TV PRESENTER Dermot O'Leary
SEXY ACTOR Jude Law
POP RUDE GIRL Pink
SKINNY ACTRESS Renée Zelwegger
HOLLYWOOD HEART-THROB Leonardo DiCaprio
BAD-BOY RAPPER Eminem
COCKNEY ACTRESS Barbara Windsor
TV FUNNY MAN Jonathan Ross
GEEKY ACTOR David Schwimmer

The Really Big Crossword
PAGE 40

The Ultimate Big Brother Quiz
PAGE 32

1a 2c 3a 4b 5b 6c 7b 8a 9b 10a 11b 12a 13c 14b 15a 16a 17b 18c 19a 20c 21a 22a 23b 24c 25b 26a 27b 28c 29c 30c

The Little Britney Quiz
PAGE 44

1b 2c 3a 4b 5a 6c 7b 8c 9a 10a

Spot The Difference — PIC B
PAGE 88

1 Woman's pen lid is a different colour
2 The text on the banner is upside down
3 The shoe in the autograph picture of Paris Hilton is a different colour
4 Man's tongue is a different colour
5 Man has no mouth
6 Paris' necklace has some of the rings missing from it
7 Paris' dress has an extra strap
8 Paris is missing a strap from her bag
9 Paris has a gold earring
10 One of the security bars, near the banner to the right of Paris, is missing

The Not-So-Big Crossword
PAGE 110

The Will Young Wordsearch
PAGE 111

Stockists

Ant & Dec: The Quiz
PAGE 120

1a 2a 3b 4b 5c
6c 7b 8b 9a 10c
11c 12a 13b 14c
15a 16a 17b 18b
19a 20b